ACADEMIC SHARECROPPERS: Exploitation of Adjunct Faculty and the Higher Education System

by

Wendell V. Fountain, D.B.A

authorHOUSE™

1663 LIBERTY DRIVE, SUITE 200
BLOOMINGTON, INDIANA 47403
(800) 839-8640
WWW.AUTHORHOUSE.COM

First published by AuthorHouse 02/25/05

ISBN: 1-4208-2366-3 (e)
ISBN: 1-4208-2367-1 (sc)
ISBN: 1-4208-2368-X (dj)

Library of Congress Control Number: 2005900817

Printed in the United States of America
Bloomington, Indiana

This book is printed on acid-free paper.

Contents

About the Book

*T*his is a nonfiction book which addresses the exploitation of adjunct faculty and the higher education system. The term "academic sharecroppers" is used synonymously with the nomenclature "adjunct faculty" because of the minimal financial and other support given to adjunct faculty by institutions of higher learning. This book is a result of the research, personal observations, and experiences of an academic sharecropper that spans nearly three decades. The issues of what is right, just, and fair are addressed relative to the failure of the academic system to properly recognize and reward adjunct faculty—academic sharecroppers. This book maintains that ethical and moral breaches by administrators in the higher education industry needs to be addressed at the societal level. Chapter one is titled "This Is the Way It Is—Believe It or Not" because of the outrageous exploitation of academic sharecroppers, students, and the general public. Chapter two is concerned with the issue of outsourcing of college and university teaching, Chapter three shows that the education industry is primarily a big business which rivals the healthcare industry. The influence of sports is highlighted and discussed. The plight of the adjunct is dealt with in chapter four. Chapter five is concerned with the efficacy of online courses. Chapter six expounds on the problems with the vagaries of student grades and the games people play. Chapter seven examines the issue of Student Faculty Evaluations (SFEs). Chapter eight provides insight into the administrative incompetence and strategic bungling of administrators in higher education. Chapter nine discusses the student customer and customer student dilemma. Finally, chapter ten is comprised of a series of vignettes experienced by the author in the execution of his teaching assignments in various geographical locations, and lastly, the epilogue contains final thoughts and reflections about the higher education system.

Ethics, too, are nothing but reverence for life. This is what gives me the fundamental principle of morality, namely, that good consists in maintaining, promoting, and enhancing life, and that destroying, injuring, and limiting life are evil.

Albert Schweitzer (1875-1965)

*To all adjunct faculty who have given so much of themselves
for so little*

Preface

After nearly three decades of working in the higher education system for many colleges and universities, primarily as an adjunct professor (academic sharecropper), because I am a business and management consultant, this insider believes there is a story that needs to be told about the exploitation of adjunct faculty, students, and the general public. This book is a culmination of observations, experiences, research, and teaching at the college/university level. Higher education, as well as the healthcare system, are out of control and have been for quite some time. Greed and insatiable egos drive nearly all decisions regarding higher education. Unfortunately, the public hardly flinches when tuition is increased. Colleges and universities, with impunity, raise the cost. For the most part, the leaders of these institutions are interested in adding programs, building physical monuments such as libraries, colleges of business, sports arenas, and so forth, while increasing the salaries of administrators and full-time faculty incrementally. Yet, the "sharecropper faculties" (adjunct faculties) seldom see any change in their paychecks. Educational institutions, whether public or private, ride the backs of their adjunct faculty.

This book is not about a veiled attempt to embarrass, deride, or criticize specific individuals or institutions, because exploitation of faculty, students, and the public is a generalized problem. Many today are quick to criticize companies for outsourcing jobs and work to lesser developed countries (LDCs). Yet, higher education in the United States accomplishes essentially the same thing by using adjunct faculty to teach courses, that is, adjunct faculty receive approximately one-quarter to one-third the pay on a per course basis as do full-time faculty, fringe benefits aside. This writing is about immorality and ethical breaches where administrative power, politics, and pettiness prevail. The following pages contain factual information and numerous real-life examples of administrative, ethical, and moral failures by leaders of institutions of higher education, where part-time (adjunct) faculty, students, and the general public are exploited.

As a colleague and friend recently said to me, "You've heard of death of a salesman, there's soon gonna be the death of a teacher." I fully realize that writing and publishing this book will probably end my stint at adjunct teaching as an academic sharecropper, but one must live by his or her beliefs. This is an accurate account of what goes on in America's educational institutions. As a teacher of business and management ethics, I'm well aware that those who whistle blow, seldom, if ever, work in their fields again. And, in my case, this is a form of whistle blowing—and so be it! Finally, if errors of omission or commission have been made, it is my responsibility and mine alone.

Wendell V. Fountain
January 1, 2005

Chapter One

This Is the Way It Is—Believe It or Not

INTRODUCTION

*W*HO ARE ACADEMIC SHARECROPPERS? They are those who share, in a very limited way, in the largesse of educational institutions—adjunct faculty. Historically, in literal terms, "a sharecropper was a farmer who was provided with credit for seeds, tools, living quarters, and food from the landowner's store. In return, the sharecropper worked the land and received a certain part of the value of the crop" (Sharecropper 1). In other words, the landowner made out, and the sharecropper barely got by. In today's world, the academic sharecroppers' world, they are used and abused. The exploitation of adjunct faculty is not illegal, but it is certainly immoral and unethical.

In ethics we teach that decisions in the workplace should be made based on what is just, right, and fair, but when it comes to adjuncts, "justness" and "rightness" and "fairness" (Hosmer 121) are thrown aside. According to authors George and John Steiner, "*Ethics* is the study of what is good and evil, right and

1

wrong, and just and unjust. *Business ethics,* therefore, is the study of good and evil, right and wrong, and just and unjust actions in business" (Steiner & Steiner 198). These definitions aside, adjuncts are nothing more than contingent workers, "field hands" if you will, poorly paid and have no benefits or workplace rights and are, with ease, expendable, making a mockery of the concept of ethics.

WHY ADJUNCT FACULTY TEACH

There are two primary reasons why adjuncts work in the system. The first reason is because of a genuine love of the teaching profession. I, and many of my colleagues, truly enjoy the interaction and intellectual stimulation of the teaching experience, while still needing the income. Another reason is because many have limited choices and simply *must* have the income—Abraham Maslow's basic need—survival. In the latter situation, it is easy for administrators to play the power and politics game without regard to fairness, because they are aware of the circumstances of these individuals. The way things are adjuncts are powerless professionals who can be and are used and abused with little or no recourse. They are men and women who give of themselves for a meager stipend without an expression of appreciation or even a simple thanks, yet essential for the survival of most educational institutions.

IMPORTANCE OF ADJUNCT FACULTY

Nontraditional education would all but be eliminated if it were not for adjunct faculty. That would mean that millions of Americans could not complete degrees all across the country. Night and weekend classes would nearly cease to exist, because traditional, full-time faculty prefer classes that are taught during normal workdays. Some full-time faculty members consider it punishment to be assigned evening classes. Further, as it is now, employing adjunct faculty is saving the educational institution enormous sums of money, because they are paid considerably less and have no fringe benefits. It is understandable that a full-time faculty member earn more than an adjunct, because full-time faculty have other responsibilities on the campus, such as serving on committees, maintaining some office hours, and conducting research, but when adjuncts earn a quarter or a third of what full-time faculty members earn (excluding employee benefits), this is the ultimate insult.

EVERYONE SHOULD HAVE A COLLEGE DEGREE—MYTH OR FACT?

One of the most formidable problems, myths if you will, in higher education is the premise that all Americans must have and deserve a college degree. They do not! What many people need is a trade or other training which provides a service or something that society needs, not a degree in psychology, business, education, et cetera. As one writer put it, "We want a mechanic we can trust . . . neighborhood bakeries . . . the barber down the street . . . a certain carpenter . . . gardeners . . . stone masons . . . not systems analysts, customer care representatives, advertising executives, and corporate tax attorneys" (Andersen 1-3).

I have had students from the undergraduate level to the doctoral level that had no business being in a classroom, but the institutions that hired me left the "weeding out" to me, because they could collect tuition for a few courses at least if not for the entire program. Some of the brightest men and women I know are without educational credentials; still, they are successful, contribute to society, and lead meaningful lives. How would we fare without builders, plumbers, electricians, and mechanics—to mention only a few? The truth is the educational system perpetuates this thinking for self-preservation. For example, does anyone really believe that certain athletes deserve or have earned a college degree? This rhetorical question is easily answered by just listening to the after game interviews.

For those typical liberal arts students who think they are intellectually superior to a machinist apprentice, it would be interesting to see how they would deal with the mathematics curriculum a machinist apprentice must master—as well as a lot of the other skilled trades as well. The American culture should embrace the fact that academic performance in a college is not for everyone, and that those who pursue other avenues of success are not less able than those who successfully achieve the awarding of a college degree. Unlike 40 or 50 years ago, today's students are practically guaranteed a degree. Educational institutions are a reflection of industry. It's all about revenue and expense. It's all about money and the bottom line. On the one hand you are told by leaders of educational institutions that you are to assign the grade students earn, but on the other hand, the truth is, if you flunk too many, *you* are the problem. As President Harry Truman once said, when confounded by conflicting economic advice, "What I need is a one-hand economist." He was tired of getting two stories instead of one. What teachers need to be told is to do what is moral and ethical in the assignment of grades—not compromise your integrity so that students can pass.

Far too many institutions of higher learning put more pressure on the professors than the professors are allowed to place upon the students. Though most educational leaders deny it, student evaluations can make or break an untenured faculty member or an adjunct. The best adjuncts do what is right regardless of the consequences. If students don't earn a good grade, they don't receive one. As a mentor for adjunct faculty for many years, I have had a number of them tell me that they were afraid to assign the real grade some students should receive for fear that they would never be rehired by that institution.

So, leaders of education not only exploit the myth that everyone must have and deserve a college degree, but they also do everything they can to make sure all students pass, regardless of performance. Later, from my personal experiences, specific examples will be provided.

STUDENT EXPLOITATION

It is common practice for colleges and universities to exploit students in as many ways as educational institutions can. How is this accomplished? Simple, just raise the cost of tuition whenever you choose, justifying it in whatever manner that's convenient. If that's not enough, raise the cost of fees or create a new fee. Once students have committed to a specific degree program, those students become captives—their choices are very limited. After 15 or more credit hours, at most institutions, it is exceedingly difficult to transfer those credits to a different institution. In some ways, educational institutions remind me of banks, because most large banks spend an inordinate amount of time analyzing and determining how to fee the exploited customer one more time.

TEXTBOOK WOES:

There are other ways to take advantage of the student. For example, charge them more for textbooks than if they were to purchase them elsewhere. Most college bookstores charge at least an additional 20% for a book. Moreover, it is a common practice for some professors to require a student to purchase a specific text and never use it. Speaking of textbooks, how about requiring students to use (in 2004) the 5th Edition *Publication Manual of the American Psychological Association*? Back in 1964 I used this publication manual when it was a fraction of its size and cost of today. A condensed version of this product has been available on the Web for years. In fact, many institutions have an abbreviated form that one can download *free* with the click of a mouse. In my estimation, with the exception of the changes necessary because of the Internet, the way it was done in 1964 is just as good as it is today, but money cannot be made unless a new product appears.

Some institutions require that adjuncts use texts authored by full-time faculty members, whether or not there is a better product available. In some cases, I've seen nothing more than photocopied materials sold, at an unrealistic price in college or university bookstores, which are required reading for students. Sometimes, students are even required to purchase dissertations published by their professors as required readings. Talk about a conflict of interest! I know this is true because it happened to me. It would be easy to hold these professors accountable for lapses of ethics, and they should be, but they are not in charge. Department chairs and others who oversee what goes on in classrooms should prevent such activities. Poor administrative leadership and management are responsible for allowing these things to occur.

ONLINE COURSES:

This practice has to be one of the greatest educational exploitations to ever grace us with its presence. Even some of the best American and global educational institutions praise this method of delivering "educational" services. Colleges and universities everywhere simply *must* have online capability. Online courses have been sold to the student population as the convenient and flexible way most students want to *educate themselves*. This is nonsense! The fact is most students don't like online courses. They prefer human interaction and the social experience of a classroom setting. Although, I must admit, I have told many of my classes over the years that, when it comes to education, students are more willing to accept less for their money than anything else they purchase. Part of the problem is higher education has become too customer service oriented and too concerned about money. Whatever a student wants, that's what the student gets. I used to think that universities should be more accommodating as well, but when I was a returning student at the University of North Florida (UNF) where I majored in psychology, I learned that I was there to be educated and not trained. My two best friends Ron and Rick, also psychology majors, and I decided we needed to have a little talk with, Dr. Thomas Carpenter, the President of UNF. We were told we had to take 35 quarter hours of venture studies outside of our major. Well, we didn't like that, so we got an appointment to see him so that we could tell him a thing or two. President Carpenter was a resolute man of distinction, and we had a great deal of respect for him. When we entered his office, he told us to have a seat. He sat back down at his desk and listened patiently to our concerns. When we were finished, in his kind but firm way, he said, "We are not here to train you, we are here to educate you. Here you will receive an education. This is not an apprentice program. Now, gentlemen, do you want to receive a degree from this institution?" Of course we all three nodded our heads. "If that's the case, you *will* take those 35 quarter hours in venture studies. Have a good day." Obviously, we thanked him, excused ourselves, and scurried to our respective classes.

I fully realize that there are those who will take advantage of online courses, because some are single parents, have work problems, or even like sitting in front of a computer screen hours on end, but what about education? Are we willing to trade an educational experience for training so that we can get a piece of paper somewhere down the road? Quality of education is the issue. And, like it or not, courses "taught" in this manner are little more than electronic correspondence courses or computer-based training (CBT).

I have attempted to "teach" two courses of business strategy at the master's level online, and those were the most unrewarding teaching experiences I've ever had. The time and energy I expended conducting this class was three or four times that of a traditional class. It seemed as though I taught each of the 16 students in the entire class separately. Once, I went away for four days during my first online class only to return to 104 e-mails from the 16 students. It took me more than six hours to answer those students, and the pay was pitiful, $100.00 per student for the course. What made it worse was the knowledge that the students were paying $750.00 each, excluding books, and I was using my office and customary overhead, computer equipment, printer, and paper. In other words, they grossed $12,000 and I earned $1,600. Believe me; by the time I finished my second course that was it. The two courses had exactly the same number of students (16 each) and my total compensation for those courses was $3,200 and the university netted $20,800.

I can't imagine ever hiring anyone with nothing more than an online degree. Before those of you who are detractors become too disturbed, let me assure you I think online training has merit, but only in a limited way. Notice, I used the term "training" because that's where it can best be applied, not education. It's absurd to assume that students receive a comparable education without classroom interaction. Then, there are those who vigorously point out that the ability to use computer chat rooms nullifies my argument. This is a ridiculous assertion. A computer screen is a cold medium of communication. Study after study has shown that the richest form of communication is face-to-face.

I would never try to invalidate the importance of technology, but the technology of today, or perhaps I should say the *affordable* technology of today, does not replace the traditional education system, yet. Educational institutions have become so market driven that if the college or university down the street is implementing online courses, then, those institutions must do it as well. Copycat strategy will not always work. Just because someone else is doing it doesn't mean that everyone else should. My best advice is to wait until the technology has sufficiently matured before developing extensive online programs and, in some cases, requiring that students register for online classes. Even educational institutions that don't offer a full menu of online courses still have blended courses, that is, classes that are both face-to-face and computer-based. Though these blended courses, in my opinion, are not the best approach, it's certainly better than all online. So much of the educational experience is missed when there is limited or no human interaction. This issue will be dealt with more fully in chapter 5.

THE TENURE SYSTEM

Becoming a full-time, tenured faculty member, in some ways, resembles a Supreme Court appointment. Even if you don't play the game anymore, it is unlikely that you will lose your position. Where in industry can anyone have assured employment? Nowhere is obviously the answer; therefore, why does such a system continue to flourish? Years ago American Airlines used to have a slogan they used to promote the company—"We earn our wings everyday." In other words, American Airlines knew that the public had a choice when they chose an airline. But, when one becomes tenured, the leaderships of educational institutions become exceedingly limited to what they can do to or with tenured faculty. Unfortunately, some faculty members become abusive to their students because of this archaic system.

For example, a few years ago I was an advisor, adjunct faculty mentor, and adjunct faculty member of a university in the mid-west. This university had many centers throughout the U.S. and even some outside the country. One of the locations was in Florida. I assisted the university in a variety of ways to get students registered and prepared for their master's program. The classes were taught on the weekends. I had advised and worked hard to fill a particular class. I went out one Saturday night to a dinner only to return home and see that I had received a raft of calls on my answering machine. I immediately began checking these calls and found that most of them were from students taking this class which I had worked so hard to fill. Generally, they were upset and disappointed in me, because of the treatment they had received in class that Saturday from a full-time professor from the campus. He had been assigned to teach the course rather than an adjunct professor, as was normally the case. What my calls to individual students revealed was nearly all of the students had been insulted by the full-time faculty member. He began the class by saying, "I really don't care if you learn anything or not. It's up to you. I'm a full-time, tenured faculty member with fourteen years of service and there's not a thing you can do to me." I verified that comment from several different students independently, so I have no reason to doubt them. Well, obviously, he decimated the class. I lost eight of the sixteen students. They dropped the course. One might think that this, in some way, did have a negative effect on his career, but not so. Because of the usual administrative incompetence, he was promoted to department chair four months later. This is such an old story but one that is usually quite accurate. Those who seem to care the least tend to excel in the promotion cycle, and that is difficult to rationalize.

GRADUATE ASSISTANTS (GAs)

When doctoral students enter their programs, they lose a lot of their individuality and freedom. Since most universities require their doctoral students to be campus bound, i.e., live and study on the campus, doctoral students become, in some ways, indentured servants. Most full-time, tenured educators who are professors at the larger and most notable institutions, have graduate assistants (GAs), also often referred to as teaching assistants (TAs). The purpose of GAs or TAs is to conduct research and teach classes for the tenured faculty responsible for a particular course and class. Graduate assistants are not generally paid much, if anything at all. They do what they are told. Recently, when I asked a new doctoral graduate if he taught as an adjunct, he replied, "No, not really, but I've been doing what I was told when it comes to teaching as a graduate assistant." And if the truth were known, that's one of the reasons traditional institutions insist that the only way you can earn your doctorate is on a university campus—they don't believe in any type of nontraditional education. They need the free or nearly free help.

I remember when I was a doctoral student; I approached a professor of stature and told him I had a great idea for a journal article. I did all the research and writing, the article was published, and his name appeared as the first author. Since he had authored dozens of books and many articles, his name had to appear first—that's the way it's done in education—so much for fairness!

If you're wondering what this has to do with exploitation of the public, let me explain. Suppose you had a son or daughter you sent to a specific college or university because of the reputation of a key faculty member who you wanted to influence your child. The fact is it's highly unlikely that your son or daughter would ever even *see* this particular professor—let alone teach your child! To further illustrate, in August of 2004 I was speaking at a gathering of business people about the exploitation of the higher education industry, and at its conclusion one of the attendees spoke with me privately. He told me that his son had gone to a university in Ohio to work on his doctorate. What his son didn't know at the time was that he would end up teaching all of his principal professor's classes. Moreover, he discovered that his principal professor was so busy working on a book, that even he couldn't get an appointment to meet with him. Out of desperation, he finally transferred from the university in Ohio to one in California where he finally completed his degree. This is not an anecdote which has little significance, because this is not an unusual situation. If anything, this is standard operating procedure.

Graduate assistants are much like indentured servants; they have to put in their time before they are released.

POWER

Nearly every college or university with which I've worked over the past 30 years has allowed administrators to demonstrate vindictiveness, play political games, and exploit adjunct faculty. Enamored and blinded by the power granted them through the institution they wield their legitimate power as the sword of a centurion. Amazingly, despite field hand wages, many administrators act as though they are doing *you* a favor to allow you to teach as an adjunct. The games range from questioning your expense reports to denying you the opportunity to teach courses for which you are qualified, just because they don't like you personally or are jealous and envious of your independence. In fact, if you show confidence and ability, many full-time faculty and administrators resent it. This resentment can become a genuine problem if you are too confident and capable (for them). As an adjunct, if students prefer you as a teacher over a full-time faculty member, you become a target, because it won't be long before you never receive another teaching assignment.

POLITICS

Many years ago, I worked for the Department of Defense. I thought at the time I was working in the most highly charged political environment one could imagine. That was before I became a full-time faculty member and administrator at a small, private university. That's when I really became aware of the political games played at the top and all levels of the organization, and I learned that promises made were not always kept by those in power. Have it in writing or forget it!

The days of honor and trust died with the end of the handshake as a symbol of commitment to agreements.

A number of years ago, I was academic sharecropping for a university with which I had had a long, solid relationship. The university decided that a leadership change needed to be made in their regional office, so the campus leaders brought in a new director who had been with the institution as a faculty member and administrator for more than 20 years. She immediately called upon me to assist her, because she was unhappy with how many of the old-time academic sharecroppers were grading major papers and projects, so she began a systematic funneling of much of that work to me. I knew that the "geriatric four" were going to give her grief— and they did.

These old hacks began their attack at the campus level by chipping away, over time, at her credibility. These disgruntled incompetents misrepresented what she had been doing to her bosses on campus, and things began to unravel. She believed in high standards of academic achievement, and these men truly resented her. It took them about a year to break her, and break her they did. The emotional pressure, lies, and personal attacks which she endured finally drove her to near collapse. The political manipulating that these men did was a disgrace. What's really sad is the fact that those who sent her deserted her, but I didn't. I did everything I could to support her because I liked and admired her for the effort she made. In the end, she became ill and finally had to leave her position and eventually had to leave the university, all because she did her best to better the program for the institution.

Just as a postscript, this lady now works for a small college as an administrator where she has found a degree of happiness and contentment. Apparently, this institution is not given to playing destructive political games.

PETTINESS

Before I became exposed to the educational environment, I'd always thought that the men and women who were terminally degreed, i.e., have the highest degree in their disciplines, were analytical, intellectual, and special. Little did I know that they could be just as human and petty as most people. I suppose that my love of education and the profession had blinded me—my idealism and beliefs were founded on myth rather than reality.

When it comes to pettiness, sometimes the administrative support staff is so bureaucratic and narrow minded, that one is incredibly challenged by these policy wonks. They can and do make your life miserable! Generally, creativity and innovation are absent from their menu of characteristics.

LOYALTY AND FAIRNESS

Loyalty and fairness are qualities absent from most of the educational institutions that employ adjunct faculty. It matters little to them how long you have served and sacrificed. There is little rationale used in course assignments. A course assignment that you often get is given to a new person without explanation. If a particular institution normally pays $2,000 for a course, that's the amount you will receive, regardless of how many years you have served them. If a new adjunct faculty member is hired, he/she will receive the same $2,000 for the course. Most make no distinction between a long-term adjunct faculty member and a new one.

My advice to those who teach as adjunct faculty is to compute the actual number of hours spent in teaching, traveling to where the course is being taught (because many of us have to catch flights and rent cars to get there – that's why we are called "Roads Scholars" or "Freeway Flyers"), e-mailing/

phoning students, writing and grading exams and papers, and responding to institutional administrators about the class you are teaching. After you have obtained the sum for those activities, divide that number into what you were paid to teach the course. The result will probably shock you. It is highly likely you will be earning less per hour than a high school graduate working in a factory or your local supermarket. What's even worse is teaching a class of MBA students who are making three to four times in their companies than what one can earn in a year teaching as an adjunct (based on adjunct pay of $15,000 per year which is on the high side). In addition, a typical elementary school teacher, on average nation-wide, is paid approximately $30,000 per year for a nine-month teaching contract. Consider this; a new elementary school teacher usually possesses only an undergraduate degree in education. That teacher is earning twice what the typical adjunct faculty earns who might be teaching at the graduate level. To add insult to injury, the typical adjunct faculty member possesses a master's/doctorate degree. How is this just, right, or fair?

For those of us who teach courses for universities which have satellite campuses, clusters, or cohorts hundreds or even thousands of miles from the main campus, we have to charge all of our expenses (car rentals, hotels, meals, etc.) to our personal credit cards, not credit cards of the employing institution. Depending on the number of classes we teach, this can amount to hundreds or even thousands of dollars within a 30 day period. Reimbursement usually takes four to six weeks. How is this just, right, or fair?

Universities which have distant operations ride the backs of adjunct faculty by not paying them any of their salary until the end of the course and final grades have been submitted. That can take from two to six months. Keep in mind that the student has to pay *upfront*, and that the university has full use of those funds for months. Those dollars can be, I'm sure are, invested in treasury bills, overnight funds, and other interest earning accounts, while the academic sharecroppers wait. How is this just, right, or fair? It's unfortunate, but greedy colleges and universities take full advantage of hard working and dedicated adjunct faculty.

Chapter Two

On-shore Outsourcing—Contingent Faculty

MERICAN BUSINESSES HAVE BEEN CRITICIZED by many citizens for their penchant to outsource manufacturing, information technology (IT), software development, and even call center work to other countries— even third-world countries. Yet, few from the public have complained about the "on-shore outsourcing" that goes on in higher education. In business it sometimes makes competitive sense to outsource, because if your competitor is paying less than a dollar an hour to someone in Indonesia, you can't continue to pay your employees $20.00 per hour plus benefits in the United States. There's just no way to make up the difference in efficiencies.

THE PRACTICE OF OUTSOURCING

The practice of outsourcing is not new. Business has always outsourced many of the services needed. For example, only the largest of firms have their own legal staffs, or engineering and construction personnel, or own financial institutions. What has changed in industry is simple; it's the number of services/functions that have increased over the past quarter of a century. Businesses of today outsource services and functions closer and closer to their core business, but there is a danger in doing so. When outsourcing of parts of the core business is accomplished, the firm loses control. The defunct ValuJet, now AirTran Airways, became victim to that mistake May 11, 1996, when 110 passengers died in a plane crash in the Florida Everglades. The subsequent investigation indicated that it was primarily the fault of SabreTech. ValuJet had outsourced the maintenance of oxygen generating canisters to them. "Investigators said the probable cause of the crash was a fire ignited by oxygen generating canisters . . . ." (CNN).

More than a decade ago, Peter Drucker, one the world's most foremost business thinkers, writers, and futurists said that anything that was not directly involved with the provision of a service or the manufacturing of a product would become a candidate for outsourcing, but he also warned of the dangers of outsourcing core components of the business. A Delta Airlines slogan states, "The most important service we can provide is your safety." This is something that ValuJet forgot.

INDUSTRY ORIENTATION OF HIGHER EDUCATION

Educational institutions are also in competition with one another, but not like global businesses—that being aside, "The buzz words in higher education are efficiency, rightsizing, accountability, and budget reductions" (Avakian 1). As a business consultant and businessman, that sounds all too familiar to me.

As budgets continue to shrink in state sponsored colleges and universities, the temptation to use more adjuncts will become almost hypnotic, the path of least resistance. Private educational institutions have it a little easier; they can just raise tuition costs, increase fees, seek greater endowments, squeeze pay increases of full-time faculty, require full-time faculty to teach more courses, and use more adjuncts. Moreover, when it comes to tuition and fee costs, private institutions outstrip public institutions significantly.

At the present, "there are more than 1,100 public and private community colleges (1,581, including branch campuses), serving more than 5.2 million students taking credit classes and an additional 5 million taking noncredit courses" (Berry 1-5). Berry went on to quote a dean from Tennessee who said that 76% of the faculty at his college were contingent faculty and that his college had one of the lowest ratios in the state. There are literally hundreds of thousands of contingent faculty across America who are considered to be second tier professors/teachers by their full-time faculty counterparts. Essentially, a class system of sorts has developed. Mike Dobson, an adjunct professor in Boston with a master's degree and author of the book *The Ghost in the Classroom,* has harsh words for college and university administrations. According to him, "They're hypocrites....If you ever hear an administrator pontificating at a commencement about equality and fairness and opportunity and work hard and it will pay off—and then you look at the people who are working hard, in their own backyard—the things that they say just ring hollow" (Delaney 2).

Greg Hodes, Ph.D., commented on a sculpture called "Still Standing" that the Johnson County Community College in Kansas City, Kansas had purchased for its sculpture garden in the amount of $93,000. "I suggest that they reflect on the possibility that the person 'standing still' next to them may well be one of live 'adjuncts' who teach most of the courses at JCCC at one-third the salary of full-time faculty, with no fringe benefits, no job security, and no sculpture garden to call their own" (Letter to *Kansas City Star* 6/20/00).

Since nearly half of all faculties in the higher education system are contingent faculty, what would happen if they all quit? As things are now, contingent faculties have very little say in anything on most campuses. Also, "It is important to note that adjunct faculty have fewer rights and protections under federal law than the lowest-paid, hourly employees working at Jack-in-the-Box!" (Suhrbur 1). Moreover, what if the millions of contingent workers in America's workforce all quit? I'm sure many would if they could, but most have little choice. Most of them are hoping for regular, full-time employment, just as do most adjunct faculty. These workers, like adjunct faculty, receive low pay and few or no benefits.

CORPORATIZATION OF UNIVERSITIES

Universities have embraced a two tier pay system much like that of global corporations. Outsourcing and the contingent worker are at the heart of this strategy, because of a need for shifting costs and avoiding litigation. In nearly every instance the greatest expense for a corporation is its human resources, and the same is the case for colleges and universities. When costs and litigation are examined, it's easy to see why Peter Drucker has stated that the human resource that was once an organization's most valuable asset is now an organization's greatest liability.

Schmid and Herman, editors of *Cogs in the Classroom Factory: The Changing Identity of Academic Labor* argue that, "in this process of 'corporatization' faculty have lost much of their authority and traditional prerogatives to make academic decisions. Accompanying this corporatization is what [the editors] refer to as the 'casualization' of higher education—and increased use of part-time, adjunct faculty and the 'outsourcing' of teaching to these 'contingent' faculty (Solidarity Forever 120).

In an article by Richard Moser titled "The New Academic Labor System, Corporatization And The Renewal of Academic Citizenship," he discussed at length the exploitation of adjunct faculty and graduate students.

It is no coincidence that the period 1972-1977 marked the first surge of and greatest relative growth in the use of adjunct faculty. We look back at the early 1970s as a time when society's existing economic assumptions, sometimes called the mid-century social contract, underwent profound revision. In higher education the changing times were, and still are, characterized by disinvestment, the ascendancy of a corporate style of management, and the subsequent shifting of costs and risks to those who teach, research and study. That meant that the faculty would be slowly transformed into part-time employees without due process or economic security and that students would increasingly carry a greater burden of the costs as higher tuition, debt and work (Moser 1).

Moser went on to say, ". . . the two or multi tiered workforce became one of the most effective strategies for realizing corporate and administrative costs. . . . The change since 1975 is striking. Part-time faculty have grown four-times (103%) more than full-time (27%)."

Barbara Wolf's 1997 video, *Degrees of Shame: Part-time Faculty: Migrant Workers of the Information Economy,* emphasizes the poor working circumstances encountered by adjuncts, i.e., last minute course assignments and the cobbling together of many low-paying courses as possible from a variety of institutions, just to make a living (Budd 1). When I began developing and writing this book, I was unaware of the existence of this video, but it is certainly reminiscent of *ACADEMIC SHARECROPPERS: Exploitation of Adjunct Faculty and the Higher Education System,* in its chronicling of the debasement and exploitation of adjunct faculty. As of 2001, part-time faculty totaled around 400,000 (Budd 5), but that number grew to an estimated 500,000 adjuncts nationwide by 2004 as reported by P.D. Lesko, the publisher of the *Adjunct Advocate* which has 80,000 readers (McArdle 3). McArdle also stated:

> *Even top-ranked institutions now make heavy use of them; at New York University, for instance, about 70 percent of the faculty are adjuncts. . . . Until recently, there were few complaints from students and parents—in large part because adjuncts as a group are as dedicated and effective as their full-time colleagues.*

Education has become a commodity rather than an experience. The University of Phoenix understands corporatization all too well with a total enrollment of more than 100,000 students and growing rapidly. They realize the value of advertising just as the pharmaceutical industry does. That's why, with frequency, we are told in television ads to ask your doctor about one drug or another, because people are asking and, ultimately, paying for the advertising costs in the price of the drug prescribed, just as students are paying for advertising and marketing costs of their educational institutions.

In a review of the book *Academic Keywords: A Devil's Dictionary for Higher Education* which appeared in *Post Modern Culture*, "An Academic Exorcism," Michael Alexander Chaney wrote the following:

> *Conversation about the lack of full-time jobs for Ph.Ds turns inevitable to the excessive and abusive use of part-time faculty or the exploitation of graduate student employees, which in turn suggests the replacement of tenured with contract faculty. . . . Without question, it is on the subject of university corporatization that we find the authors achieving a level of indignation*

> *comparable to any radical manifesto . . . . The book's objective is not to dictate a fully formed agenda, but to inform and to raise consciousness: to shock us out of our apathy* (Chaney 1-4).

One can only hope that when enough of this information is disclosed, the deep sleep of Rip Van Winkle will be abridged, because this issue is not exactly a hot topic at a cocktail party. Many have suggested that structural causes account for much of the problem, that is, there's too many Ph.Ds being produced. "Why not produce fewer Ph.Ds and reassert control over the market by reducing the labor supply . . .? The simple answer is that many administrators would rather let the students teach one another before they'd surrender any market power" (JUMP CUT 2). As a side note, I find the suggestion to produce fewer Ph.Ds almost humorous in light of the annual creation of 10,000 surplus lawyers by the educational industrial complex, but that doesn't stop law schools from enrolling as many as they can, especially when there are more than a million attorneys currently working in the legal system.

ADJUNCT OUTSOURCING

If Adjunct faculty were working in lesser developed countries (LDCs) or where costs of living are significantly lower than in the United States (fully realizing that this is an international problem), perhaps an argument could be made for the low pay and absence of benefits. But the adjuncts I'm speaking of live and work in the United States where the cost of living is equal to or greater than other developed nations, Both full-time and adjunct faculty buy groceries, fill their automobile gas tanks, get hair cuts, and buy houses in the same neighborhoods. Both pay taxes, live, play, and worship in the greatest country in the world, so why should adjunct faculty be treated so differently? What about being treated as an equal to full-time faculty in the governance of the institution for which adjuncts work? They, too, are stakeholders and should not be viewed as second-class citizens who have different needs than full-time contract, non-tenured track, or tenured track teaching professionals.

WHAT ADJUNCTS WANT

Adjuncts only want equal treatment based on their contributions to the educational institutions for which they work. They want equal pay for equal work, retirement savings, better administrative support, more lead time to prepare for a course, and a closer adjunct to permanent staff relationship. The bottom line is adjuncts want to be involved in decision making and the educational system in general.

In a quality of work life survey conducted at George Mason University in 2000 (George Mason 1-2) adjuncts made the following selected comments when asked, **"What has been a source of stress for you at George Mason?"**

"Poor compensation for adjunct faculty. This gives the impression of injustice and unfairness."

"Not knowing if I have a class to teach until the last minute."

"Parking, especially for 1:30 classes."

"Not having university help at all with savings for retirement."

"An irritation has been that graduate teaching assistants are paid more than adjuncts. That says, 'We're really glad to have adjuncts because they reduce our teaching load. They save us money on salary. We don't provide them with space or benefits. Our lucky students can have instructors who aren't worth much!'"

When asked, **"What has been a source of satisfaction for you at George Mason?**

"GMU gives me the opportunity to teach, which I love."

"Interested students who always attend class, ask questions and make the class challenging and exciting."

"Being able to take a course tuition-free."

"Facilities – classrooms and meeting rooms are well kept and generally meet teaching needs – tv/vcr, computer, etc. Either they are there or are easy to get (well, not if you are an adjunct/student)."

My primary research practically mirrors these comments of adjuncts at George Mason University. Over and over again, I've heard these statements during the past 30 years. As a business consultant the one thing I have found to be an overarching issue, one that usually bothers employees the most, is unequal or unfair treatment.

Moral and Ethical Considerations

Not long ago I was speaking to a group of Rotarians in north Florida about the issue of adjunct faculty exploitation. Though I had opened many eyes to the injustices that go on in higher education, one gentleman completely missed my point. His response was, "No one puts a gun to their head. They don't have to teach if they don't want to." He totally disregarded the just, right, and fair thing that should be done about those who teach as adjuncts, regardless of an adjunct's motivation. Moral and ethical treatment should be of preeminent concern to all who employ anyone, especially the highly educated among us. If those who are responsible for teaching the philosophical stances of such giants of the classics as Plato, Socrates, and Aristotle, and then disregard the philosophical, ethical, and moral positions of these great thinkers, where is our moral compass and who will show us the way? One could turn this into a religious discussion, but many would not listen or, in some cases, be insulted by the teachings of Christianity; however, if one did test this from a Christian point of view, I cannot imagine Jesus Christ treating people so selfishly and shabbily.

Miller Solomon, an English professor at Auburn University, described the situation as, "It's a pool of cheap labor for the university. But ethically, it's a shame." Features writer Elaine McArdle interprets it this way, "Adjuncts are being exploited by cost-obsessed colleges, he [Solomon] and other opponents to this trend maintain. They say that part-timers are overworked, given no voice in college governance, and may lose their jobs if they're tough graders or take controversial positions" (McArdle 3). All of us adjuncts, in varying degrees, have had to deal with this in some manner. The power, politics, and pettiness of administrators and their administrative staffs can be incredibly insensitive and abusive, all because adjuncts have no legal standing in the colleges and universities for which they work. Since those in charge operate with this knowledge, they live by the letter of the law, while ignoring the spirit of the law. If the spirit of the law was their guiding light, adjunct faculty would receive just and fair treatment. Ethics is about doing the just, right, and fair thing, not necessarily only the legal thing.

The following exact wording is indicative of how some colleges and universities try to cover themselves legally when it comes to a contractual agreement between the university and an adjunct faculty member. <u>This offer, if accepted, and any other contracts as yet uncompleted, constitutes the University's only employment agreement with you and in no way do they promise or imply any future offers or ongoing commitments beyond the stated term(s)</u>. In fact, the wording was added after a long-term faculty member had challenged the administration when they refused to issue him any additional contracts, and they could not provide a reason why he was denied further involvement with the institution.

According to the AFT Executive Committee Minutes: May 4, 2001, of the Community College of Allegheny County located in Pittsburgh, Pennsylvania, Roger O'Toole, a board member, asked the college's attorneys about the maximum number of credits per term an adjunct is allowed to teach, because he was concerned about what would constitute full-time employment. "The College's attorneys advised ten as the most to assign an adjunct without giving full-time temp status with benefits. The official number is ten but exceptions can be made for eleven or twelve credits to allow three classes for 4-credit sections" (AFT Executive Committee Minutes: May 4, 2001). Once again, the concern was about what was legal and not necessarily what was just, right, or fair.

CONCLUSIONS

Exploitation of adjunct faculty is shameful, and as long as it never becomes a societal issue, the educational industry will continue with business as usual. The fact that people are unfairly treated and compensated means nothing to the leaderships of colleges and universities. The concern of most is the letter of the law, while disregarding the spirit of the law. It's noteworthy to take into account that society saw fit to pressure legislators decades ago to ensure that, when it came to the sex of an employee, men and women should earn equal pay. The Equal Pay Act of 1963 (later amended in 1972) was created to fix that problem, but when it comes to adjunct faculty (academic sharecroppers); we are left out in the cold. Educational institutions follow the letter of the law, and so they are protected. Admittedly, some unethical employers still find ways around the law, but women today are being paid closer on a par with males. The most recent data I've found indicates women are earning $.75-$.80 to the dollar of what a male earns.

Finally, God forbid that an educational institution foul up by allowing academic sharecroppers to be considered to be full-time employees. If that should ever happen, those people would actually have to be paid benefits. Then, how would these colleges and universities financially survive? One thing that might help is the cost savings realized by not having to market and advertise on an incessant basis. Some of that money could even be used to better compensate the academic sharecroppers who play a major role in helping those institutions fulfill their missions.

Chapter Three

Big Business—The Higher Education Industry

*T*O MANY PROFESSIONAL EDUCATORS this is an abhorrent assertion that higher education is big business, but face it, it is! In the early part of 2004, as an adjunct, I was teaching a doctoral course in Washington, D.C. While there, I learned of a proprietary university owned by a group of investors who had determined that they wanted a revenue increase of 40-60 percent for fiscal year 2005, so the full-time faculty and adjuncts were given their marching orders, i.e., make sure that more new students are registered and current students are retained. These same four or five top lieutenants of the university had pocketed millions the previous year, while pressing the full-time and adjunct faculty for productivity increases, translated that meant doing more for smaller or no pay increases. But, the millions the top managers and administrators received the year before wasn't enough—they had to have more. Since this was a proprietary university, one might wish to dismiss it, because private universities have to make a profit. So let's

29

look at the public higher education system of North Carolina. According to Dennis Markatos, Guest Columnist of *The Daily Tar Heel,* from 1990 to 2002 tuition had increased over 150 percent . . . . "Admittedly, raising the price of public education is a national trend . . . many excuses are used to justify a vote for tuition increases. A classic reason is that professor salaries are too low" (Markatos 1). He went on to say that tuition hikes were blamed on everything from Hurricane Floyd in 1999 and the budget deficit in North Carolina to the economic recession of 2002. As Markatos stated, it is a national trend and Michael Arnone concurs that tuition and fees for 2003-4 have been increased significantly (Arnone 6). Table 1 illustrates some of these national increases.

Table 1

	2003-4 tuition and fees	Percentage increase over 2002-3
U. of Arizona	$3,593	38.6%
U. of California system	$5,437	29.5%
State U. of NY system	$4,350	27.9%
U. of Oklahoma	$3,741	27.7%
U. of Virginia	$6,149	19.1%
Ohio State U.	$6,474	14.3%

Source: *The Chronicle of Higher Education*

The Higher Education Economic Boon

In an article which appeared in *The Sun Herald* November 6, 2002, David Tortorano wrote, "Higher education is big business in Mississippi, and it's not good business to cut funding for an industry that's growing" (Tortorano 2). He further stated that, "[The] University of Southern Mississippi is a $250 million business that receives about $76 million annually from the state. . . . It brings in more than $60 million in external funding for research, and the goal is to increase that to $100 million by 2005." This is only one educational institution in Mississippi. What about the University of Mississippi, Mississippi State, and all the other colleges and universities of Mississippi? Extrapolate this number to the rest of Mississippi and then to the entire nation. If this doesn't constitute big business, what does?

The economic boon created by new and continuing students has far-reaching effects. Every year when colleges and universities crank up their educational engines, businesses of all types benefit. The restaurants, bars, banks, credit unions, gas stations, coffee shops, merchant malls, etc., are all positively affected. Education is a powerful economic driver. Experts in the Department of Labor of the state of New York say, "Their [students] tuition dollars and creative energy help fuel the entire region's economy. Higher education is one of the fastest-growing industries in Central New York, and it now rivals manufacturing as the primary source of new money coming into the community" (Eisenstadt & Weaver 1).

There are many large and small educational institutions in cites and towns across America which are the primary economic drivers. For instance, the University of Florida, the largest university in the state, is the heart and soul of Gainesville, Florida. Where would that city be without the University of Florida? It would be hardly more than just another tiny rural town like so many others in the state.

Another example is Central Michigan University, one of the smaller universities in the state, located in Mount Pleasant, Michigan. Mount Pleasant *is* Central Michigan University. The economic relationship of these educational institutions to their communities can be likened to that of certain military installations. Fort Polk, a Readiness and Training Command of the U.S. Army, is located in Leesville, Louisiana, and Leesville has a population of about 8,000. By comparison, Fort Polk, the military installation, boasts of more than 33,000 soldiers, so the fort has more than four times the number of military members than there are citizens of the town. Where would Leesville be without Fort Polk? The point is if it were not for colleges and universities around the country serving as primary economic drivers, there are many cities and towns like Gainesville, Florida or Mount Pleasant, Michigan that would either cease to exist or struggle for a meager survival.

THE RESEARCH BOON

Collectively, colleges and universities all over America are recipients of billions of dollars for research grants from local, state, and the federal government, not to mention the revenue brought in from the private sector and philanthropic foundations to conduct research for profit and not-for-profit organizations. A case in point is the Iowa State University Research Park. "A study by an Iowa State University researcher suggests that the ISU research Park's substantial and diverse economic activity bolsters Iowa's economy" (Iowa State University 1). The author specifically stated there was a direct link "to almost $88 million in total industrial output." Another example is Pittsburgh, Pennsylvania where: there is a direct link in that Pittsburgh's future increasingly hinges on its research and foundations.

During the 1980s, Pitt tripled its sponsored research from $51million to $150 million, mostly

*in health and medicine. During that same
period, Carnegie Mellon quadrupled its research
from $29.1 million to $122.6 million. . . . .The
University of Pittsburgh Medical Center ranks
as the largest employer in the region, Pitt is sixth
and Carnegie Mellon 19th. In addition, . . . it's a
maxim of higher education that every $1 million
in research accounts directly and indirectly for
31 jobs* (Zlatos 2-3).

It was reported in fiscal year 1998 that a patent explosion was evident, because there were 11,784 new discoveries. "The deluge in discoveries has translated into a healthy revenue stream for universities. Research universities earned $725 million on the royalties and other income derived from the patents, up 19 percent from 1997" (Cohen 2).

Governor Jeb Bush of Florida understands the economic effects of research and research institutions. In October of 2003 he called for a special session of the legislature to pursue economic development. "Bush and Dr. Richard Lerner, president of the Scripps Research Institute, said at a news conference the state will set up a $310 million research facility for Scripps . . . ." The hope is that over the next 15 years university research on a host of diseases such as Lou Gehrig's (ALS), AIDS, diabetes, other onerous illnesses will be researched until cures are found (Tallahassee Democrat 1-3). Bush also announced the creation of another $190 million "mega-fund." Both the Scripps funding and the "mega fund" were part of a $900 million federal gift. Research has become so important and lucrative that many educational institutions are hiring greater numbers of low-cost adjunct faculty so that the full-time faculty can devote more of their time to conducting research which enhances the bottom line. "There may be short term benefits and savings from this strategy, but over time students, faculty, and the institution are all the losers in this vicious cycle" (Bricault 8).

Business and educational institutions worldwide have formed or are forming partnerships which have mutual benefits. There's nothing wrong with such partnerships, but educational institutions must not lose sight of their purpose, that is, training is for business and education should be left to colleges and universities. Training is about the skills needed to do specific things in a work environment, while education is a holistic approach to human development, where one is taught how to think not what to think. Training teaches us what to think, how to perform a specific task, or to behave in a certain way. Montana State Senator Jim Elliott has put it this way, "Education is the fundamental economic driver that provides health care, employees who can read, write, and think, and the success of business ventures large and small" (Elliott 2).

THE BIG BUSINESS OF COLLEGE ATHLETICS

High profile, collegiate sports such as baseball, basketball, and football has become <u>America's new religion</u>, not to mention professional sports of all types. Essentially, college teams are the farm teams of their professional counterparts, where only the best of the best make it to the "Bigs." But, before that small percentage of college players get to the professional level, those college stars, regardless of the particular sport, are responsible for millions, and sometimes tens of millions of dollars, of revenue for their educational institutions. But, what about, at best, the 95% of collegiate sports figures who are never drafted by the pros and don't get millions of dollars in signing bonuses and multi-year contracts worth tens of millions? What happens to them? Universities exploit them until they are injured and can't play anymore or graduate them without a genuine education. How sad. But this is what happens to athletes who befall injury that ends their careers as athletes who have eyes on a future of millions of dollars. To illustrate just how poor some educational curricula are, as reported by *The Washington Post* and the *Weekly Standard* regarding a course titled "Coaching Principles and Strategies of Basketball," a sample of the questions from an exam for the course is as follows (see Exhibit I below).

Exhibit I

How many goals are there on a basket ball court?
a.1 b. 2 c. 3 d. 4
How many points does a 3 point field goal account for in a basket ball
game?
a. 1 b. 2 c. 3 d. 4
How many halves are there in a college basket ball game?
a. 1 b. 2 c. 3 d. 4.

In a report issued by a member of the U.S. House of Representatives dated March 11, 2004, the following statement was made, "I submit that students taking courses like this were cheated out of an education" (The Committee on Energy and Commerce 2).

In 2000 the University of Oregon announced an $80 million expansion plan for the football stadium. As professor of English, James Earl, put it, "An athletic program that prospers while academic programs starve is a warning sign . . . We're an institution of higher learning, not an arm of the entertainment industry. Our mission statement makes no mention of sports or entertaining the community" (Earl 1).

For the first time in its history, Kansas University's chancellor is paid less than the athletic director who was hired in June of 2003. The chancellor is paid $275,000 and Lew Perkins, the athletic director, is paid $400,000 per year. Further, "Perkins then hired four new staff members and gave them salaries of more than $100,000 [each]; a fifth is making $95,000."

Perkins has also indicated that, "KU's athletics department had equipment and facilities needs totaling $70 million to $80 million" (Rombeck 3).

During football season, the economic boon for communities across America is huge, when compared to the impact of athletic budgets of higher educational institutions. The University of Arizona is a typical example. When home football games and basketball games are considered, along with fan spending, it is estimated that "the combined total for 2004-5. . . could reach an estimated $75 million or more" (Tenser 2). To further illustrate, I was in Jacksonville, Florida on the 26th of October 2004, and heard an interesting news report on WOKV (690 am) radio. The story addressed the estimated economic impact of the annual Florida-Georgia or, depending on your team preference, the Georgia-Florida football game. The reporter stated that the game would have an estimated direct economic impact of $7 million and an indirect impact of an estimated $20 million for the greater Jacksonville area. This is only one game! This doesn't include the economic impact of the annual Gator Bowl game which is held after the regular season at Jacksonville in Alltel Stadium. That game should have an even greater economic impact.

It appears that big business is the reason for much of the spending on sports. Tim Goral of *University Business* wrote, ". . . the fact that college sports have become big business for many schools, a business built on a sports economy that rivals that of some Third World Countries," (Goral 2) we have this out-of-control situation. He further stated:

> *The CBS television network . . . paid $6 billion for exclusive rights to air the annual March Madness basketball series for the next 10 years, and ABC has a $525 million, seven-year deal to show the four college football Bowl Championship games. Teams that make it to the top bowl games can earn nearly $13 million each.*

Not only is big business and big money an issue at the university level, but even conference levels, at least in football, have become problematic. In 1991 the Florida State Seminoles opted to join the Atlantic Coast Conference (ACC), which raised a lot of eyebrows at the time. But the ACC is looking for the big television money, that's one of the reasons they are courting the Miami Hurricanes. Of course, the Big East leadership is not happy about the possibility of loosing their centerpiece in football, but it looks to be inevitable. "With Miami on board, the ACC could pretty much write its own ticket with regards to a television package that would not only be enormously lucrative for every school involved, but also put the ACC right up there with the Big 12, Big Ten, and SEC in terms of national viewership" (Haynes 2).

MANIPULATION OF VALUES AND STANDARDS:

The so called "arms race" of intercollegiate athletics, especially at the Division I level, has escalated to heights never before seen. Hungry sports programs must be fed if teams are going to be able to compete. There is a great temptation for coaches and recruiters to say and do whatever it takes to attract the best high school players in the country. When a team suddenly propels to the top of its sport, most of us are not usually surprised when we hear that that team has been judged to have violated the rules of the National Collegiate Athletic Association (NCAA). Over the past 20 years, there have been a number of teams in basketball and football which have violated NCAA standards.

In 1984, the football program of the University of Florida was put on probation for NCAA recruitment violations. It was reported at the time that the head football coach, Charlie Pell, and his staff were responsible. In 1989, Joe McGuff, Vice President and Editor of *The Kansas City Star* and *times* reported that:

Three of the conference schools currently are on probation, one has just come off probation, and another is under investigation. Three members of the Colorado football team have been charged with rape, and seven others have been found guilty of charges ranging from assault to misdemeanor menacing. Three Oklahoma players have been charged with gang rape, one player shot another in the athletic dormitory, and Charles Thompson, the Oklahoma quarter back, has been charged with selling cocaine. Nebraska is being sued by a former faculty member who claims she was dismissed when she was too diligent in checking on the athletes' grades and their attendance at class (McGuff 1).

Since this is 2004, one would think that things would have gotten better since 1989, but not so. The University of Alabama and many others have had their problems, too. Florida State University and the University of Miami are well known for the lack of character among many of their players, but the coaches just look the other way or take only symbolic action. Many of the things described in the quote above by McGuff have occurred in both of these schools. The stories about problems with players of these educational institutions seem endless, but it is not only those two universities, it is a problem of epic proportions throughout the intercollegiate system.

Why does this situation exist? Failure to uphold moral and ethical standards are often a result of incredible intercollegiate competition. Winning means money! Losing, if you are a Division I college football coach, just might mean you get fired. I'm sure Ron Zook of the University of Florida can attest to that, because he was sacked in the middle of the 2004 season. Since some "football power" universities routinely pay salaries in excess of a million dollars per year, a coach doesn't want to lose a multi-year contract. Coach Bobby Bowden of Florida State University was the first college coach to hit the million dollar mark at $1.5 in 1995, and by 2001 Steve Spurrier, then of the University of Florida, topped out at $2.1 million (see Table 2 below).

Table 2

Top 10 Millionaire Football Coaches of 2001

$2.1 million	Steve Spurrier	University of Florida
$2.0 million	Bob Stoops	University of Oklahoma
$1.5 million	Bobby Bowden	Florida State University
$1.45 million	Mack Brown	University of Texas
$1.3 million	Barry Alvarez	University of Wisconsin
$1.3 million	Phillip Fulmer	University of Tennessee
$1.3 million	Glen Mason	University of Minnesota
$1.25 million	Tommy Tuberville	Auburn University
$1.2 million	Nick Saban	Louisiana State University
$1.2 million	Rick Neuheisel	University of Washington

Source: *USA TODAY* 8/3/2001

The above list is not exhaustive, because there are an additional 13 other coaches in the million dollar range which includes notables such as Pete Carroll of the University of Southern California and Joe Paterno of Penn State University (Wiesberg 2). As of January 2004, Bobby Bowden's salary was raised to $2 million and Bob Stoops went up to $2.2 million (Drape 1-2). There seems to be no end in sight. The salaries of these coaches do not represent the total income they will receive during the years. We haven't even addressed the issue of speaking fees and commercial endorsements.

As a result, values and standards sometimes become a problem for the athletic director and/or the coach. "The big business/big entertainment model of college athletics is increasingly incompatible with the values and purposes of higher education. . . . We are in a battle between the values of higher education and the reward structure of big time athletics programs" (Leland 1-2).

Years ago I was an administrator and faculty member at a university which was competitive in baseball and basketball. It was not uncommon for the coach to call me about a player in my class. The calls would usually come about 3-4 weeks before the end of the term. Though I never thought I received unreasonable pressure, I did feel pressured. For example, the coach might say, "You know how important Bobby is to the team, and I'm concerned about his grade for your class." I usually handled it well, because I knew the pressure the coach was under, but I never compromised a single time. That was not always easy for me, because I had a great deal of affinity and respect for most of those players and the coaches, but I always believed that academic standards are academic standards and that they must never be breached. Unfortunately, many of us who have tried to keep the standards up have had difficulty in doing so because of exceptions and loose academic standards of colleges and universities. Bob Smizik, a sports columnist, wrote in the *post-gazette* of Pittsburgh, Pennsylvania in 2001:

> *It wasn't that long ago that most major universities treated their athletes like students and accepted only those who could measure up academically. The few schools that did not were branded as outlaws. But nowadays, they're all outlaws. There's not a school in the country*

that won't make an exception for an athlete and that goes for the Ivy League and the service academies (Smizik 1-2).

The net effect is that college athletics is damaging the integrity of the educational system, because the players are not student athletes they are athlete students. College football and other collegiate sports are big business for universities, where students, players, coaches, faculty, boosters, and a host of others are manipulated and exploited all for the sake of revenue. So, it's not only adjunct faculty who are exploited within the higher education industry, but it's the entire industry. It is being used for that which it was never intended.

CONCLUSIONS

It is without question that the higher education industry is truly big business. All costs from tuition to books and fees have escalated on a par with the healthcare industry. The research boon and the athletic programs produce revenue streams that are the envy of some of the best businesses in the United States. The economic impact of a prominent educational institution creates a tremendous ripple effect throughout the local economy that surrounds it. This is especially true of athletic programs—football and basketball in particular. In the case of the former, we now have at least 23 college football coaches in the millionaire category and the latter, basketball, is closing fast. This is all happening while the professors who are delivering the educational service and experience are being paid pathetic wages, and at this point I'm referring to full-time professors. What academic sharecroppers are earning is embarrassing. It is the height of exploitation. The hotdog and beer vendor in the stands of a football game probably earns more on an hourly basis than an academic sharecropper. It's a sad commentary about the American society, but education, religion, sports, and everything else seems to be about money.

Chapter Four

The Plight of the Adjunct—No Way Out?

*T*HE PREVIOUS CHAPTER HAS CLEARLY SHOWN that the higher education industry is little more than a self-serving, self-absorbed big business, where intercollegiate football coaches are earning enormous sums of money. The facts are most Division I coaches are receiving multimillion dollar contracts which are typically ten times that which chancellors and presidents of educational institutions receive on an annual basis. If it were not for educational institutions, there wouldn't be sports programs; coaching jobs would not exist. The truth is these head coaches are being paid salaries that rival CEO salaries of many American corporations. I would be hard pressed to find anyone who enjoys college football more than I, but education has been lost, manipulated, and exploited.

The educational industry is feeding on itself. What's more it's all about bad leadership and bad management. From a strategic perspective, taking the path of least resistance is a short-term solution which has long-term, negative consequences. As a business strategist I can easily see that dark days are coming. Since adjuncts are already teaching approximately one-half of all courses taught in higher education, and that number is growing, isn't it obvious that a day of reckoning is looming? The lack of moral resolve and fortitude that is needed to correct this "separate but equal" (with a wink) condition is astounding. Yet, administrators leading many of American's most revered colleges and universities ignore common decency and continue to perpetuate moral, ethical, and economic injustice. Somehow the purpose of colleges and universities has been lost and is now supplanted by financial concerns and athletic programs. Education has become a secondary issue. Now, keeping costs down and active sports programs up are what matters.

On September 25, 2004, it was reported by *Fox News* that some students are being held back in middle schools so that they will be able to compete at a higher level in high school and college, i.e., they will be stronger, taller, and have more experience at playing their sport. The example given was a middle school child who wanted to play basketball, so his friends went on to the next grade while he stayed behind. This type of unethical behavior goes on while head coaches are earning millions; nearly one-half of all professional educators (adjunct faculty) are earning tip money in the world of a head coach (maybe $15,000 a year).

The plight continues. Richard Fulton, dean for instruction, at Whatcom Community College in Bellingham, Washington, said:

> *It's a lousy way to make a living say the critics, and those people caught in what seems to them to be an endless cycle of short-term, part-time employment complain about it with mounting bitterness. An increasing number of their tenured colleagues, too, criticize colleges and universities for turning a blind eye to what is to many a regressive, unethical practice that strikes at the heart of academic quality* (Fulton 1).

It's interesting to note that the last concern Dean Fulton mentioned was academic quality because, for the most part, the research indicates that adjunct faculty perform at a quality level equal to traditional full-time faculty. To illustrate, David Slavin, visiting assistant professor of history at Knox College, Galesburg, Illinois, has taught at a number of universities, including Temple and Rutgers, sees it as follows:

> *Ironically (and predictably) adjuncts do as good a job teaching as tenure-stream faculty, but are hamstrung by heavy load, lack of continuity, contstant distractions of job searches, etc. The quality of their teaching masks the two-tier structure. But students and their parents are being had, and adjuncts have an enormous power to disrupt the system just by advertising that fact . . . . we have the power to embarrass the academic power structure morally and politically. We give the lie to all the talk about commitment to teaching and to education in general. The more the plight of adjuncts is exposed to the public at large, the harder is it for administrators of higher education or tenure-stream faculty to remain morally credible in the public arena* (Slavin 4).

This problem is not going away anytime soon, but the day will come when administrators, leaders, and managers of educational institutions will have to confront their conscious or unconscious contempt for the men and women who have dedicated themselves to quality teaching, while being treated as though they are second-class citizens who are powerless and have little or no standing in their institutions.

WHERE TO NEXT?

Mostly it depends on your life's circumstances and/or where you want to be. In my case, at sixty years old, I'm headed into the sunset of adjunct teaching (academic sharecropping), particularly after this is published, but my hope is to do what I can for those who will continue to fight the good fight and those who will follow me. For people like me, it is too late. We wandered into this thing called adjunct teaching, liked it too much to quit when we should have, and allowed ourselves to be used and abused by the powerful and the petty. I have no regrets. I have enjoyed my teaching experiences in spite of the power hungry, cost cutting administrators, annoying underlings, jealous full-time faculty, and policy wonks that make you as miserable as they can, when they can, because they can.

I would like to recognize many other professionals, both adjuncts and full-timers, with whom I've worked as an adjunct over these years, but it would not be politically wise to do so. Many of them still have careers about which they care, and for me to align myself with them, would do them great injustice. However, they know who they are, and I salute each and every one of them. I will always consider them as my friends. But, where do we go from here? As Slavin said, ". . . we have the power to embarrass the academic power structure morally and politically." I agree that is a possible course of action, but to do so means that those who lead the educational industry have the capacity to morally and ethically change—to me that remains a question. So, what other recourse is available?

TIME TO ORGANIZE?

As a business consultant, my advice to my clients has always been, "If you don't want a union, don't give your employees a reason to have one." At this point, the problem is so intransigent, there might not be a better option than to collectively come together and organize on a national basis. With numbers of more than 500,000, these are voices that can and should be heard. Will it be easy to accomplish this task? Hardly. If one takes a look back into the 1920s, when unions were at economic and working condition war with businesses, no one excepting the delusional could ever think that this will be a buttery slide.

Since 1969, when unions were 24 million strong, membership has steadily decreased to today's current level of less than 16 million. There are several reasons for the decrease in membership. America is no longer a manufacturing giant; we ceded that to the Chinese, just as we gave up steel manufacturing during the late 1970s to the Japanese. The soul of unionism was formed in the world of manufacturing, i.e., working conditions, benefits, and pay. Manufacturing in the U.S. economy has been in a freefall for more than 30 years. In fact, manufacturing now makes up only about 25% of the total economy and is declining. We are now "service" America.

Another factor which has played an important role in union membership decline was the quality movement of the 1970s. Many of America's large employers began treating employees better as a way to sell the concept of product and service quality improvement; thereby, undermining some of the traditional issues of unions. Also, the downsizing, rightsizing, and restructuring of corporate America's workforce has created employment uncertainty, accompanied by a larger and larger contingent workforce which has had an effect on membership. Further, unions of the 21st century have become unpopular. Many blame unions for the economic ills of the country. If blame were to be placed, I would assign that to poor leadership and management of corporate America. Never forget, unions have never gotten anything that management didn't give them. Back in the old days, the early 1970s, when American corporations had little or no competition, lazy management just continued to give and give and pass price increases on to the consumer. That can't be done today because, the U.S., globally, has all the competition it can handle.

Though this book is about the exploitation of adjunct faculty and the higher education system, and not about unions, the reader needs to understand my personal philosophy regarding unions to gain appreciation for my belief that a national union might be the solution. I have had to rethink my philosophy regarding adjunct faculty because of the injustices perpetrated on good men and women slaving in the fields of academia.

When I was a young man working in a mattress factory in Jacksonville, Florida, I had my first taste of union pressure. Out of the more than 100 employees employed there, I was the only one, who was not management, who refused to join the union. Since I was a rugged individualist, I believed that I could fight my own battles. Besides, I viewed that particular union to be owned and operated by management; therefore, ineffectual as a representative of the workers. Even the company management came to me and asked me to join the union. Finally, they sent the vice president of the union, who was located in Atlanta, Georgia, to Jacksonville and personally request that I join. A long story short, I can still see his 1964 Thunderbird burning rubber as he flew out of the parking lot in disgust.

About 20 years later, I was working for the United States Navy as a civilian in a quasi-human resource position, where I found union leaders to be unreasonable about many things. One thing that bothered me greatly was the time we filed the necessary documents to dismiss one of their union members who worked in the Production Department of the Naval Air Rework Facility of the Naval Air Station located in Jacksonville, Florida, and the president of the union disagreed with our action. The employee in question had been found guilty of drug running and stealing government property. He was tried, convicted, and sent to Raiford Prison in Starke, Florida. Our rationale for the dismissal was abandonment of the job. He had just begun serving a four-year sentence, so we needed to hire another aircraft painter. The union president confronted me and the Director of the Production Department and told us we had no right to fire this man. He said, and I quote, "You have no right to fire him, because if he could be here, he would. He's being held against his will." Now, if this isn't a case of unreasonableness, I don't know what one is.

Finally, about five years ago, I actually joined a writers union, because I thought that perhaps I could learn about writing projects and potential work that Hollywood and others had to offer. But, that also was a disappointment. I found it did me little good to belong, so I stopped paying dues. What is my position today on being a union member? If I could join a national union which represented adjunct faculty, which has real teeth and clout, I'd drive or fly wherever to the union headquarters and proudly sign up and encourage every adjunct (academic sharecropper) to do likewise. Though I still see myself as a rugged individualist, I fully realize that we can't go this alone. Adjuncts must attack this problem as a monolithic group of professionals, because as individuals there is little we can do. The reason is clear; we adjuncts are powerless and serve at the mercy of unprincipled men and women of the higher education system. These are people who have little or no conscience and lack a moral and ethical foundation. They care only about themselves.

A parallel to this individualism versus collectivism option is our national defense system. Individually we cannot protect ourselves against the terrorists who hate and do whatever they can to kill us. We have no choice but to depend on our national defense system and Homeland Security. Without the Department of Defense and Homeland Security, we would soon be overrun by these evil, cowardly maniacs.

EFFORTS TO ORGANIZE

There are ongoing efforts to organize adjunct faculty, but there's a lot of piecemeal activity. As things are now, we adjuncts are divided and conquered. We work in every state of the union for colleges and universities all over, where we have little or no influence or standing on an individual basis.

Even full-time faculty supports the unionization of adjuncts. In a poll taken in 2003, an overwhelming majority, 86% of full-timers, voted yes as opposed to 14% who voted no regarding support for adjunct unionization (Kaye -1). If for no other reason, full-timers need to support this effort, because as it is full-time faculty positions are eroding. Ultimately, the end game is to break the union. One could surmise that if a 75% or more adjunct faculty base ends up teaching most of the courses at educational institutions, the union will become very vulnerable. Administrators and managers at colleges and universities will be in the driver's seat. Once that happens, the union is lost. Full-timers will find themselves to be nothing more than contingent workers as the adjuncts are now. They, too, will become academic sharecroppers. One Adjunct living in Virginia said it well, "I won't be too surprised if in ten years university faculties are composed of one or two full-timers who teach a course or two and handle primarily administrative functions while the remaining members are adjuncts" (Atkinson 2).

Tom Suhrbur, IEA organizer, of metropolitan Chicago where there are thousands of adjunct instructors working at more than 50 colleges and universities has developed a strategy to combat the problem. "Instead of a campus by campus approach focused on a collective bargaining campaign, we must first create a metropolitan-wide organization, recruit members and, only when we achieve a critical mass on a given campus, campaign for collective bargaining (Suhrbur-2). He then suggests all adjunct faculty would be eligible to join the Adjunct Faculty Association of Chicago (AFAC).

Elizabeth Chernow of George Washington University reported in the March 11, 2004 issue of *GW Hatchet,* the campus newspaper, "Adjunct professors filed a petition Monday to bring a union to campus, following almost two years of failed attempts at gaining representation. Professors are calling for benefits, job security, and higher salaries" (Chernow 1). She also reported that, "GW currently has 1,115 part-time faculty members and 807 full-time faculty members." That amounts to slightly more than 72% of the faculty who are part-timers. Obviously, most of those part-time faculty have other jobs where they get good pay and benefits, so they don't need or want representation; thereby, making organizing extremely difficult.

> *In the state of Arizona some progress has been made. For example: State colleges have more than 8,000 adjunct faculty members, and up to 50 percent want to teach full time . . . Those numbers are part of the reason adjuncts are having success organizing statewide for the first time. Another is that communicating is easier by e-mail, so adjuncts are sharing information about a problem of national scope – Washington state added $20 million last year for equity for part-timers, and adjuncts in other states have been successful in obtaining benefits* (Sandal 1).

Unless a national union movement takes the country by storm, or federal legislation forces the leaders of the education industry to change their ways, it could take decades for adjuncts to achieve parity. Other than that, the education industry would have to undergo a miraculous, moral and ethical epiphany—which is highly unlikely.

FALSE EXPECTATIONS

Many, such as the 50 percent of adjuncts of the Arizona state system, want to be full-time faculty, but according to the literature, that's not what usually happens. As David Slavin so aptly put it:

> *It is the hiring process for tenure-stream positions that tenure-stream faculty most actively participate in perpetuating the adjunct system. Departments conduct searches in total disregard of institutional disadvantages suffered by adjuncts. Assumptions stigmatizing long-term adjuncts are a particularly cruel form of Catch-22: search committees demonstrate a consistent preference for recent or & 'freshly-minted' PhDs. . . . To make matters worse, nationally competitive fellowships for junior faculty often have age-of-degree requirements that gradually squeeze out of eligibility while precluding our being competitive for senior-level fellowships* (Slavin 3).

According to Alan Frey, Community College Consultant, even though administrators have had the opportunity to evaluate an adjunct faculty member and are able to assess performance over time, they usually hire someone else (Frey 1-2). The book *Ghosts in the Classroom: Stories of College Adjunct Faculty—and the Price We Pay* points out how that adjunct faculty are ignored in the hiring process:

> *Again and again, these adjuncts are passed over when permanent or tenure-track positions do open up; they are seldom regarded as colleagues by permanent faculty; they are often viewed as less than worthy even when they take*

on extra projects, advising, or mentoring; and they act professionally and generously even when their institutions not only fail to reward them for their contributions, but actually penalize them (Dubson 1).

From my viewpoint, I can certainly relate to this account. In the late 1980s and early 1990s I taught two courses of business policy and strategy every semester for four years at a southern university. Though I didn't want or need a full-time position, I was asked by the department chair if I would be interested in a visiting professor position. Because of my consulting business, I had some concerns about the time factor, but he assured me that it would not interfere with my work off campus, so at his urging I made formal application. That was a big mistake, because after the dust settled, I never taught another class at that institution.

What I found out was that some of the tenured faculty resented me. Since I had little contact with them professionally, I just didn't know how much. Later, I remembered when the department chair called me one morning at my office to make a request. He said, "Wendell, when your new classes begin tonight I want you to rattle your saber." That was not my style, so I asked why he wanted me to attempt to frighten the students. He went on to tell me that, because of my reputation as a good teacher, many of the day students were not registering for the classes taught by two other full-time, tenured faculty, and that he wanted me to, "put the fear of God in them," so that they would withdraw from my classes and enroll in the day classes taught by these professors. Those professors only had eight or nine students each, and I had 30 in each of my classes.

Though uncomfortable with the request, I did as I was asked, but not one student in either of the classes withdrew, so I called him the next day and told him what happened. He thanked me, but I could tell he had a problem. The problem, I discovered later, was that these two faculty members had records of my grades pulled, so that they could find out if I was "giving away" grades. To their chagrin, they found out that my grades were reflective of theirs. So, obviously, when they saw my application to become a visiting professor, a hue and cry ensued that forced the department chair to select someone else for the position and never hire me again, despite the fact that my student evaluations were superior to the full-time faculty. But, this is human nature and those who are insecure, easily intimidated, and petty usually win out when you are in a powerless position. It was just as well, because I was only paid $1,500 per course and, as any good teacher knows, evaluating the work of 30 students in a class is quite an undertaking.

JUST THE FACTS

This book is not about creating a mindset of victimization or pity-me-please, because me and my sharecropping colleagues are used and abused. It's about providing the reader with factual information. It's about doing what's right, just, and fair, regardless of budgetary constraints and escalating costs. Some of us have had enough. We are not going to continue to give and give to an ungrateful higher education industry, which seems to be bereft of compassion or a sense of decency.

The public has been more than repulsed by the unethical practices of corporate America over the past few years; yet, no one even sees the parallel between the egregious actions by the leaders of such companies as Enron and the leaders of the higher education industry. Corporate executives at Enron exploited their employees by encouraging them to invest in the company stock while . . . "top managers were enriched by tens of millions of dollars as the financial fortunes of Enron declined" (Steiner & Steiner 668), by taking advantage of the commitment and dedication of those employees. The leaders of higher education are just as guilty of such moral and ethical failures; it just doesn't get the press. The malignant tumor, unseen, which lies undetected beneath the skin and, without notice, quietly steals life from the body. The evil exploitation of adjuncts, students, and the general public is culturally endemic and indigenous, as long as it goes unseen, undetected, and unchallenged.

Chapter Five

Electronic Correspondence—The Online Boondoggle

*A*NYTHING BUT A POSITIVE SPIN on this insidious practice raises the hackles on software vendors, legislators, administrators of higher educational institutions (Moy 3), and some teachers of technology. This is not only a cash cow, but it has become a sacred one as well. The purveyors of software who support this electronic delivery system are prime stakeholders who care more about making money than the educational experience. Their interest is their bottom line, corporate profits, bonuses, and other forms of remuneration. I'm not saying that their interests are bad; the problem is that quality education is subordinated to selfish needs and desires of these stakeholders.

In a general sense, legislators are lazy by nature, because they don't want to take on anything which might cause them to be defeated in the next election. Their worries are about taxation, budgetary constraints, and their careers as politicians—not about what is best for education, the state, or the nation. So, when confronted with building more physical facilities which house the functions of education or the electronic delivery of information, they opt for the easy way out. Everyone out there fire up your computers! Let your mouse begin! No more, land, bricks and mortar, just clicks, space bar taps, and an electronic server.

Most administrators are an interesting lot. They sweat out every nickel or dime spent, while doing everything they can to fill the classes. As leaders and managers they act more like corporate executives of an IBM, Disney, or General Motors, where the price of the company stock and corporate profits dictate the decisions and accompanying strategy of the business. They, too, look at the bottom line and quickly realize that they can staff courses with adjunct faculty for a fraction of the cost of hiring full-time professors, because adjuncts, like myself, are not a dime a dozen, we are a *nickel* for a *baker's* dozen.

Tenure-track teachers, contract teachers, part-timers, and adjunct faculty who sing the praises of online courses are stakeholders, too, in the system. A system where, if the administration wants you to teach you are going to do it, not so much because you want to, but because continued employment is a determining factor. In other words, most of these professors simply have no choice if they want to keep a job. Online courses, electronic correspondence, have become so entrenched in the education industry that there's no going back. At some point in the future, electronic delivery of educational services will become an acceptable delivery system, but not in its present mode. All this may be a moot point because, if Peter Drucker's 1998 prediction is accurate, there won't be large university campuses in about 30 years. "Predictions are that by 2004 more than 100 million Americans will be taking part in adult education programs, many of them combining distance learning with shorter on-site courses" (Distance Learning 1).

The Efficacy of Online Courses

Current research does not make it clear. It seems to depend on the researcher's point of view. If the researcher has a positive view of online courses, then the courses are as good as or better than the traditional classroom approach; however, if the investigator has a dim view of online courses, that, too, comes out in the literature. As I indicated early on in this book, online courses are not the way to go if quality of education is the goal. If quality training is the goal, then there is some support for its efficacy. For example, "Safetylogic's Online Employee Training E-Solution has proven successful in reducing training costs while improving the transfer of knowledge to employees . . . learn faster . . . retain more . . . and save money" (Safetyologic. com 2). Just keep in mind that these results were determined by a software vendor but, despite that, I have personal experience with computer-based training (CBT), and I found it to be efficacious. I have also had experience with "teaching" a couple of online courses and found them lacking in quality of education—training, yes—education, no. This, among some of my other hypotheses, was reinforced by my research at the Academy of Management in 2004.

Academy of Management Annual Meeting

While attending the Academy of Management (AOM) meeting in New Orleans, Louisiana, August 6-11, 2004, I interviewed a small sample (26), of the attendees at random regarding online courses and other issues. There were more than 5,000 professors in attendance, some of whom had experience with online teaching. I had intended to interview a greater number, but I didn't want to inconvenience the participants, because they were there for a different purpose;

however, I did learn a lot from those whom I did interview. I only asked 12 basic questions (see Exhibit II below).

Exhibit II

INTERVIEW QUESTIONS

1. Are you a full-time professor? Yes____ No____ If so, where_____
2. Do you teach as an adjunct professor? Yes____ No____As an adjunct, what college or university?

    _____

3. Do you teach only as an adjunct?
    Yes____No____ If so, what college or university?

    _____

4. In your opinion, based on the number of students in your classes, do you believe you are fairly compensated as an adjunct instructor? Yes____ No____
5. Do you believe that class assignments, as an adjunct teacher are fairly determined? Yes____ No____
6. Have you experienced unfair treatment by administrators where you teach as an adjunct? Yes____ No____ or have you observed such treatment of others?
7. Do you believe that power and/or politics plays a role in you being selected to teach a specific course as an adjunct instructor? Yes____ No____
8. Do you teach online courses as an adjunct? Yes____ No____
9. Do you believe students receive (as good as), (better), or (worse) education from online courses?
10. As an adjunct online teacher, is it (more) or (less) work for you than the traditional classroom setting? How about the students? (more) or (less)?
11. Please estimate the percentage of students, you encounter, who really prefer online courses_____

12. Do you receive the same pay for an online course as you do for a classroom-based course? Yes___ No___ (more) or (less)

FINDINGS:

Most of the interviewees were full-time professors (20 of 26) and 18 of 26 also taught as adjuncts at various colleges and universities across the country. A majority (19 of 26) of those who taught as adjuncts did not believe they were fairly compensated based on the number of students in their classes. When asked about fairness in the assignment of classes as an adjunct, most of the respondents (17 of 26) thought that the classes were fairly determined. Regarding unfair treatment by administrators, 12 of 26 of the respondents believed that they had experienced unfair treatment themselves and/or had observed unfair treatment of others in an adjunct role. Slightly under three-fourths (19 of 26) believed that power and/or politics played a role in being selected to teach a specific course(s). Only 11 of 26 of the respondents taught online or blended online courses, and 10 of the 11 believed that students received a worse education. All of them believed that it was more work for the instructor and the student than the traditional classroom, lecture format. When the respondents were asked to estimate the percentage of students they have encountered who prefer online classes, their response was telling (0% to 20%). As far as compensation, most (6 of 11) received the same pay for online courses as they did for traditional courses.

Admittedly, this was not a comprehensive effort, but the responses certainly reinforced my thinking regarding exploitation of adjunct faculty and students. To illustrate, I've heard many administrators extol the virtues of online courses, "because students want convenience and flexibility," but the overwhelming majority of students I have had discussions with don't like online courses. I have had many students tell me, after taking an online course, that they would never do it again, because it was too much work and too frustrating. As stated earlier, the literature is mixed.

THE ONLINE EXPERIENCE

Convenience and flexibility are the words used frequently regarding online instruction. According to Myers School of Online Learning:

> *Online classes are just as demanding as the campus classroom. You still have to read the textbook and assigned class documents; you still have to follow a syllabus, hand in your assignments on time and do well on any quizzes or exams you may need to take. The difference is the face-to-face interaction with your instructor and classmates. You trade the convenience of mandatory attendance in a campus classroom for independent, self-motivated study* (Myers Online 1).

It's important to note that the problem of security is not mentioned, that is, how does anyone know who's actually at the keyboard? What about the exams, quizzes? Who's taking them and how are the exams and quizzes proctored? "How can instructors of online courses ensure that students do their own work? The answer is that, with current technology, they can't" (Botsch & Botsch 2). Some institutions require that students come in and sit for exams, but many do not, because that defeats the purpose of an online course.

In some ways, this is like a take home exam, which I don't give students, because I see them as a waste of time. I remember when I was an undergraduate student and opted for a take home exam when given a choice. I spent the entire weekend trying to answer questions, using the textbook exhaustively, and to this day, I have no idea why or how I received a grade of B.

That was sort of like the time my academic advisor and professor of social psychology looked around the room on our first day of class and proclaimed, "Guys, you all are going to have a very difficult time earning an A in this class, but you girls are not going to have a problem at all." I couldn't believe he actually said it, but, worse, he meant it. I found that out firsthand when I had a solid A going into the final week, and he held my paper in his right hand, and in a "weighing" fashion told me, "That feels about like a C," as he tossed it on his desk. The long story short of it, I did get an A, but I took a risk to do it, I challenged him. What he did then was take four books from his bookshelf and then told me, "Summarize these by tomorrow morning." I spent the entire night summarizing the four books in typewritten form, using an old manual typewriter, and was waiting for him at his office at 9:30 A.M. the next morning when he unlocked his door. Much to his surprise, I handed him the busy work he forced on me. He didn't even give me the courtesy of looking through my work, he just "weighed" it again and tossed it on his desk and said, "You'll get your A."

Though there are peculiar situations which occur in education as described above, not everyone sees the online experience as being peculiar or less educational. In one study of an advanced computer science course the material was delivered in two formats—online and face-to-face in a classroom. In both of the sections the students earned an equivalent grade of B+. "Both the online and face-to-face students reported that they were satisfied with the course . . . and the content material provided on the course website . . . . The online students used the web resources substantially more than the face-to-face students" (Wilson 2).

In this instance, I think it is important to note the type of course—a course in computers. Logically, it would follow that an online course of this nature would do as well as a face-to-face course. There are situations, based on course content, in which the online methodology works, but the type of course just described is uncomfortably close to a training experience rather than an educational one. What I have found is that courses philosophical or theoretical in nature don't lend themselves well to the online format. As an example, many colleges and universities teach organizational behavior, organizational theory, business ethics, or business policy and strategy online. The courses just mentioned need human and face-to-face interaction for optimal efficacy. In fact, most college level courses need human interaction. According to elearnspace.org, "Courses like public speaking and in-person type practicing are not easily adapted to online. However, with creative alternatives (and high speed connection and a $30 web cam) students can develop those competencies" (elearnspace.org 4). Perhaps, that's so, but I have often said, as a student, that I learned as much from my fellow students as I did from the professor and/or the required readings.

When the performance of an Internet and traditional classroom course in consumer economics was compared, Johnson et. al (2002) discovered, "that the online students scored significantly higher than those students in the traditional classroom setting on the posttest, even after controlling for significant pretest differences." The researchers went on to indicate that the students taking the course online . . . "spent 6-10 hours per week working on the course while the traditional classroom students reported working only 5 hours per week or less" (26). They also indicated that the novelty of the Internet could account for some of the extra time spent on completing assignments.

There is evidence that faculty prefer web-enhanced courses. A poll conducted in Lynnfield, Massachusetts by WebCT, the world's leading provider of e-learning systems for higher education, indicates a "faculty preference for web-enhanced classroom instruction over either traditional classroom-only instruction or online-only distance education."

The poll also indicated that, "Faculty . . . say student learning achievement is maximized in courses that combine online and classroom elements" (Distance-Educator.com 1).

There are those like myself who believe that a number of factors must be considered if an online course is going to be optimized, e.g., course content, type of student, and method of interaction (Kindred 6). Some have even suggested that personality type should be considered by professors who teach online courses to ensure student satisfaction. Accomplishing that is more than difficult, it is nearly impossible, because many people are diametrically opposed to such social engineering. They resent being characterized as having a specific personality type. Daughenbaugh, et. al (2002) used the Keirsey Temperament Sorter (KTS) as their personality identifier. KTS is like an abbreviated form of the Myers-Briggs Type Indicator (MBTI), using 16 different personality types as a measure of personality identity.

FINANCIAL IMPLICATIONS OF ONLINE COURSES

Although, development and delivery costs are considerable, the Internet is a money-making tool:

> *The Internet will offer a chance to make real profits from education, while offering students a choice about who will educate them and at what price. There's big money for universities that understand that the Net is more than a 21st-century equivalent of the filmstrip* (Phillips 3).

There have been efforts to estimate the cost of design and development of online courses. One formula developed was based on a typical three semester hour course, e.g., "How many hours of online learning make a three-credit course? . . . based on the traditional model of a campus course: using a formula of two hours of study outside class for every hour in class" that equals 135 hours. Normally, 45 hours of in class time and an additional 90 hours of outside work is what it takes to complete a three-credit course; however, the 45 hours of class time is the time needed for design and development of one online course (Boettcher 1). Although redesign and redevelopment needs will occur over time, generally, it will not require nearly the same number of hours as it did during the initial effort, so costs should decrease incrementally. Boettcher also stated that a second online developed course will take less time when done by the same faculty member.

Obviously, actual dollar costs will vary significantly for developing online capability. Much will depend on the existence of an appropriate infrastructure. If a college or university has previously invested in sophisticated hardware and software programs, costs will decrease, but otherwise costs are going to be significantly higher. That's why costs of developing the capability to provide for online courses range from $50-100,000 (Downes, 1).

Though some suggest that the student will realize a savings and consequently will benefit because of not having to travel to attend class, not having to give up their earning potential, and that institutions will pass on savings as online offerings get cheaper (Downes 3), others see hidden costs associated with online courses. For example, students might be charged for an application fee, higher out of state tuition, non-residency fees, preferential online student charges, a university fee, course fees for development costs, distance learning support, laboratory fee, internet provider fee, late payment fee, graduation audit fee, late graduation fee, and additional transcripts fees (About Distance Learning 2-3). Something to consider is that usually there are costs associated with convenience and flexibility in just about every product or service that the consumers uses. I can see no reason why the provision of online courses would be exempted.

OTHER SIGNIFICANT ISSUES

It has been suggested that as online course programs displace traditional classroom courses that teaching loads will be comprised of a certain number of students and instructors will be compensated based on the number of students they teach (Downes 2). This approach is applied to full-time and adjunct faculty. You may be assured that full-time faculty will or are earning far more per student than adjunct faculty. Further, in some cases online development time is being deducted from sabbaticals. For example, Mr. Smith at Los Rios Community College has been pressured to put his accounting courses online. According to college policy, the extra time he [Mr. Smith]

> *takes to develop the online courses would come out of his sabbatical. But Mr. Smith argues that sabbaticals are meant to benefit professors, Not administrators . . . . As president of the Los Rios College Federation of Teachers, a faculty union, Mr. Smith has tried unsuccessfully to get extra pay and time off for professors who develop and teach online courses* (Carnevale 1).

There are many concerns about the teaching of online courses. What about capping the number of students a professor should teach in a single class? Obviously, professors are concerned about what that number might be. From my personal experience, I found that 16 graduate students were nearly impossible to satisfy during the term, as I discussed in chapter one. Yet, a recent survey indicated that the cap should be 28 students (Vilic 2). As a professor, I can't imagine attempting to "teach" a course with this number of graduate students, but college administrators understand how to exploit the labor of full-time professors and adjuncts alike.

To make matters worse, what about profit seekers; those who see the business of education for what it is? Junk bond king Michael Milkin and Paul Allen, co-founder of Microsoft, see educational maintenance organizations (EMOs) for what they are—incredible money-making schemes equal to the healthcare industry. They believe that they can transform the system/industry into the next healthcare sector. They view the $700 billion education opportunity as rife for harvesting (Werry 2). Organizations/institutions such as "UNext (part of the Knowledge Universe), KaplanCollege, University of Phoenix Online, Jones International University, and over 400 new companies entering the online learning marketplace" (3) see dollar signs everywhere. Once again, we get back to money, and in the final analysis everything gets reduced to the bottom line and dollars and cents, while online course enrollments are escalating at incredible rates. This all leads to profits—not necessarily educational quality. All I can say is thank God I received my education when quality and high standards were of preeminent importance—despite a few awful professors which I endured.

Chapter Six

The Vagaries of Student Grades—
Games People Play

*I*N THE PREVIOUS CHAPTER THE VAGARIES of online courses and the exploitation of the higher education system and faculty were discussed. This chapter deals with the problems of higher education grading and the system of student performance evaluation. The problems of grade inflation and manipulation abound in a system that is exploited by one and all, that is, students, faculty, and administrators.

The following anecdote should illustrate just how serious and pervasive some of these problems are. A few years ago, I was teaching a graduate research methods course for a northern university. I had 14 students in the class and was teaching this course as an adjunct faculty member on a military base. Overall, the course went well and most of the students earned a B or better in the class; however, there was one woman in particular who did not do so. She earned what I thought to be, at least from the numbers, a generous C+.

After she received her official grade, she called me at my office to question the grade. I explained it as best as I could, but she was not satisfied with my reasoning. So, I told her that the university did have a policy in place which allowed her to grieve the grade if she were so inclined. And, I also explained that her grievance would only be sustained if the university were to find that I had graded the class in a capricious manner. She said, "Dr. Fountain, I only need one point to get me to a B-minus, and I would appreciate it if you would give it to me." Of course, I had no grounds upon which to "give" her another point. She said, "I don't want to have to grieve this grade just for a point, but if I have to, I will." I told her that I was disappointed that she thought she needed to, but if that was what she wanted, then go ahead. Well, she did grieve the grade and after six weeks of investigation by the university, which included me having to answer many questions in responding to the director of the program, they concluded that there was no evidence of capricious grading and that the grade of C+ would stand. At this point, one might assume that this was over—not so.

A few days later she filed a racial discrimination suit against me—she was an African-American and I'm a Caucasian-American. Of course, the discrimination suit more than disappointed me, because I've never assigned a grade based on anyone's race, sex, age, national origin, etc. I have always prided myself in being objective, at least as much as anyone can be, in the grading process because it certainly is not a science, and I have always given every student the benefit of the doubt. She said that I didn't like her because she was an African-American who wore dreadlocks.

Obviously, the university took this charge very seriously, as they should have, and launched an investigation of my 13-year record of teaching as an adjunct with them. This investigation took eight weeks, and during this process a three-way conference call was set up in which the student, the director of the program, and I had a conversation. I was conducting a strategic planning conference in St. Augustine, Florida, when this conversation took place. We all were on the phone at 8:00 A.M., and I knew I had to resume my meeting for the planning conference at 9:00 A.M., so I was under some pressure. Despite that, the call took place. It was one of the most humiliating experiences I've ever had in the teaching business. That student never called me by my title or even my last name; she only referred to me as Wendell, my first name. She was vitriolic, accusatory, and disrespectful to me during the entire one-hour conference call. She insulted me in every way she could, and the useless, incompetent director of the program never intervened. Two days later I called the director of the program and told him how I felt about such a humiliating experience, and I also told him that would never happen to me again, because I was never going to fall prey to such a three-way conference call.

Though I was fully vindicated in both the grade grievance situation and the discrimination charges, and spent an enormous amount of my personal time answering these unfounded claims, I never received one penny of payment for my extra work. As I expected, the HR department found that I was one of the best professors and most popular adjuncts that taught for them, and that the vast majority of students really seemed to connect with me. But, that's the way most of these pathetic colleges and universities are, they just exploit, use, and abuse academic sharecroppers/adjunct faculty in whatever ways are necessary and expedient. One of the things I've learned about administrators in higher education is that administratively most of them are incompetent, that is, they do whatever is necessary to protect themselves without regard for others.

MORE STUDENT GAMES

In the mid-1980s I was teaching a human resource management course in an Executive MBA Program. One of my students was from Sweden and a very likable person. He turned in a research paper to me at the end of the course in which I found evidence of massive plagiarism. Plagiarism is an ethical violation which has always greatly troubled me. I made sure I collected a number of the sources which he used where I could show him some of his word-for-word lifting of other authors' ideas and statements, and then I called him in for a conference. When I confronted him with the evidence, he proclaimed, "Dr. Fountain, I've always done my papers this way. That's the way we do them in Sweden. All during my undergraduate degree no one ever said that I was wrong." Of course, I didn't believe that for a moment, so I explained what he was going to have to do if he wanted to stay in the Executive MBA Program. He had turned in the paper about three weeks before Christmas, so I ruined his holidays. I gave him 30 days to prepare an appropriate research paper or otherwise I was going to the director of the program and have him dismissed. Obviously, he didn't want that to happen, because his company was paying for his degree, so he joyously complied. I told him that no matter how good the new paper was, he could not earn better than a C for the course. Just after the holidays, he submitted his paper and received his C.

Once I was teaching a Master's of Science course in Fayetteville, North Carolina. The course was held on the base at Fort Bragg. I had one female student who did every thing should could to avoid doing the work required of her and the rest of the class. She came in late on a regular basis, including lunchtime, and complained frequently about everything. She became very upset with me the day of the final exam when she came in late from lunch to take the exam and the time was half over. She pled ignorance to the time I had assigned for the final and said that it wasn't fair. As kindly as I could, I told her she would have to complete it in the time allotted as did all of the other students. When the time was up, I collected all the exams.

As the students, including her, were completing the evaluation forms on me, I waited outside the classroom. As her classmates emerged from the classroom, I said goodbye to each of them. When she came out, she said she needed to talk with me. I motioned her over to the side of the hallway, and she said, "Dr. Fountain, I don't want to talk out here, can't we go into an empty classroom?" I complied and we went to the classroom adjoining ours. After we entered, she insisted that the door be closed. Several months before this incident, university officials had warned adjunct faculty about being alone in a room with someone from the opposite sex— especially with the door being closed, so I refused to let her close it. My gut told me to beware. She was not happy about that, because she said, "I don't want others hearing what I'm saying."

To this day, I don't believe she was seeking confidentiality at all, I believe she was planning on setting me up. I could just see her tearing at her blouse and yelling as she ran from the room for the military police. They would have held me for civilian authorities, and I would have gone to jail. Obviously, I don't know this for sure, but you would have had to have been there to fully appreciate my belief. I say this because a number of her classmates said that she played games in every class, and I should not put anything past her, and that they were glad someone had finally dealt with her. Although, later, I did get a call from the director of the program wherein I had to defend my actions and even amend her grade at the director's behest. This particular student is not representative of most of the students I have had over the years, but she certainly ruined my teaching experience relative to that class.

In another incident, I was teaching an MBA marketing course for a school in south Florida in the late 1980s when I was surprised by the behavior of one of my students. It was a very large class of 29 for which I was being paid a whopping $2,000 for teaching five weekends over a ten week period (I should be ashamed of myself and I am). I had worked hard preparing for the class, and was excited about teaching marketing, because I've always enjoyed it and it was a part of my work as a business consultant. This class began at 1:00

P.M. on Saturday afternoon. I had been busy writing on the white board and lecturing for about an hour when I noticed a large opaque cup sitting on a student's desk. I didn't like the looks of what I saw, so I stopped, walked over to him and said, "Either that's urine in that cup or it's beer, which is it?" He was somewhat surprised at my question and he began stammering, "Well . . . uh . . . it's beer." I said, "Young man, either that beer or you are going to leave this class right now, which is it going to be?" Fortunately, he chose to get rid of the beer and stay in the class. For the rest of the term, with that class, I had problems. In my opinion, most of them were yuppies, too young, and inexperienced to be in an MBA program. But the greedy university for which I worked wasn't about to let that get in the way.

I could go on and on with anecdote after anecdote about the games students have played with me over my career in teaching, and later I will use other examples to illustrate how the adjuncts (academic sharecroppers), and the higher education system are exploited, but now I need to turn to the research regarding grade inflation and how the higher education industry exploits the system for its own gains.

Does Grade Inflation Exist?

Despite a handful of detractors the research is clear, grade inflation is a fact. There are a number of reasons why this is occurring; for example, adjunct faculty and full-time faculty fear student evaluations of their performance, some professors are "dumbing down" their courses to be popular so that students will pass, administrators and faculty have less headaches when students are happy, some professors are just not making their courses challenging enough, elite schools and others want to make sure that minorities and others can graduate/social promotion, company education reimbursement policies, and finally, it's about revenue stream—the student-consumer philosophy. Colleges and universities do whatever they can to make sure that the money keeps rolling in by passing marginal students with A's and B's.

GRADE INFLATION:

For those who disagree that grade inflation is a problem, speak with officials at the University of Arizona. According to one account, "Grade inflation at the University of Arizona has become a matter of serious concern . . . . No longer do students receive recognition corresponding to their achievements. Those who earn A's and B's are indistinguishable from those who receive them as a courtesy" (Penner 1). In addition, from 1991 to 1998, graduating seniors' GPA's went up.

In my experience with students, if they earn a C in an undergraduate course, they believe they are complete failures. Professor Steve Falkenberg of Eastern Kentucky University agrees with me, "Students receiving grades of C or less feel the instructor has evaluated their performance as less than satisfactory" (Falkenberg 1). I have a C or two as an undergraduate on my transcript that I would gladly trade for any A I ever earned, and I earned my share. Unlike many students today, I found some courses I completed to be extraordinarily difficult. I also found that in those courses I performed at a satisfactory level which is a C. For example, I earned a C in physics, and that's a C that I'm very proud of, because I had to have an A on the final to pass. The professor and *I* had difficulty believing I was able to rise to the occasion.

Stuart Rojstaczer, a professor at Duke University, collected data on 34 colleges, and he certainly believes that grade inflation is a problem.

> *[He] hasn't given a student a C in more than two years, and he finds himself giving plenty of A's. He is the first to admit that he is part of a nationwide problem of grade inflation, but he says that the only way to change things is to*

> *get universities to work together to deal with the issue. . . . The latest wave of grade inflation started around the same time that colleges began operating more like businesses . . . treating students like customers who bring in revenue. Today, students and parents demand high grades, and professors are reluctant to buck the trend* (Young 1).

Even Harvard University has the problem. Harvey Mansfield, a professor of government, at Harvard believes that the grades being assigned are scandalous. "The grades that faculty members now give—not only at Harvard but at many other elite universities—deserve to be a scandal" (Mansfield 1). Professor Mansfield has even developed a two-grade system, i.e., one for the public record (registrar) and one in private which represents the real level of the student's performance, because the system is so fraught with inflation. In a *USA TODAY* article by Mary Beth Marklein she stated that, "At Harvard University, a recent study found that nearly half of all grades awarded were A or A-minus. . . . A tenured professor is suing Temple University, saying he was fired because he wouldn't make his courses easier or give students higher grades." She further indicated that some of the blame for grade inflation was as a result of, "An administrative response to campus turmoil in the 1960s, and a trend, begun in the 1980s, in which universities operate like businesses for student clients. . . . She added that "the advent of student evaluations of professors and the increasing role of part-time instructors" played a role (Marklein 1).

John Merrow, a scholar-in-residence at the Carnegie Foundation for the Advancement of Teaching, views grade inflation as a major educational issue. He reported in *Carnegie Perspectives* that:

> *These days it seems as if nearly everyone in college is receiving A's, making the Dean's List, or graduating with honors. . . . In a study for the American Academy of Arts and Sciences, former Harvard Dean Henry Rosovosky found that in 1950 about 15 percent of Harvard students got a B+ or better. Today, it's nearly 70 percent. . . . Eighty percent of the grades at the University of Illinois are A's and B's and 50 percent of Columbia students are on the Dean's List* (Merrow 1-2).

Assistant Professor, Jonathan Dresner, of the University of Hawaii at Hilo has identified the nexus between grade inflation, accreditation and review, and assessment. According to him, "Grade inflation (and its primary/secondary equivalent, social promotion) has made grades and advancement difficult to rely on as a measure of academic success. . . . Grade inflation has three primary causes: student culture, pedagogical culture and institutional culture" (Dresner 2). This really is the crux of the matter. Academic sharecroppers like me and full-time faculty have a professional, moral, and ethical obligation to do our duty and assign the real grades students earn, regardless of the consequences.

Jay Halfond, Dean of Boston University's Metropolitan College, agrees that students have come to expect high grades, but the reaction to grade inflation might not be a victimless crime, because he points out that Ivy League schools attract the top one percent in the country (Halfond 1). What about these bright, exceptional people? Should an artificial ceiling or grade curving be put in place just to mirror the national average? That was done before and it wasn't right then and it won't be right now. The brightest and best students should not be penalized for the transgressions of the higher education industry.

Some students at Boston University are already beginning to feel the effects of grade "deflation" and are complaining about it. They see the performance of their peers at other universities, where those students are doing less and making better grades than they, and those students see it as unfair treatment (Pelletier 1). Like most things, we tend to overreact and, this time, it will be at the expense of bright, hardworking students, creating an unjust condition.

THE EFFECTS OF CORPORATE POLICY ON GRADE INFLATION:

Even corporate education reimbursement policies can create unnecessary pressure to inflate grades. As an academic sharecropper, I have been pressured time and again by good and honorable students to assign a higher grade than that which they earned, because they needed the money so that could continue with their education. The reason they gave was that their company reimbursed them on a sliding scale, i.e., if they earned an A they were reimbursed at 100 percent, a B at 75 percent, and C at 50 percent. This is an absurd policy! Logically, it makes no sense. We don't cut an employee's pay in half when he/she receives a satisfactory performance appraisal (which is average, a C). The employee continues to be employed as a contributing, productive worker. Besides, it is unrealistic and unfair to expect an employed married man or woman with children and family responsibilities to compete with traditional college students who have far more time to study together and discuss class materials.

When I was Chairman of the Human Resource Committee of the Board of Directors of VyStar Credit Union a few years back, I tackled this ridiculous policy. After educating the other members of the Board on the unfairness of the policy, from an adjunct faculty viewpoint, we passed a new policy that to this day provides for 100 percent reimbursement for a C grade or better. In addition, since then, we added cash awards for those who completed two-year, four-year, and master's degrees in recognition of their achievement. We understood and appreciated the sacrifice our employees had to make in order to earn those degrees.

FINAL THOUGHTS ON GRADE PROBLEMS

To begin with, it is nearly impossible to be completely objective. My philosophy has always been to minimize my subjective inclinations by looking at and evaluating the student's performance rather than personality, looks, likes, or dislikes. I have interacted with a number of students over my career who didn't like me and I didn't like them, but my job was to be objective and fair in assessing their work, and I believe that I have done so honorably.

Also, it is irrefutable that grade inflation exists. There's just too much evidence of the problem. Even as I was putting the final touches on this book November 12, 2004, I heard a *Fox News* report about Benedict College in South Carolina where two professors were fired because of their objections to giving away grades, that is, in this case students received 60% of their grade for just showing up. The report indicated that even if they failed all of their exams, they would still pass (*Fox News* 11/12/04). Moreover, not only is the literature replete with account after account, but from my own observations in the higher education industry, I have no doubt that the industry is feeding on itself by exploiting students and faculty so that revenue streams will be increased, not decreased or interrupted. Students, parents, and employers expect to get their money's worth, which translates to higher grades. As discussed in chapter three, education is big business. If grade inflation continues, a high grade point average will have no meaning. Society will no longer be able to use it as a measure of success.

I actually worked for one institution which made sure students graduated. If they didn't pass in my class, an administrator would arrange for a tutorial for the same course to be administered by one of their favored political, academic hacks so that the student would pass. Notwithstanding, the student still had to pay again for the course. Those of us who believed in high standards caused those administrators a lot of discomfort as the exploitation of the system continued.

Chapter Seven

Student Faculty Evaluations—Who's In Charge?

*A*S THE 1950S CRUMBLED UNDER the weight of the cultural meltdown of the 1960s, changes which questioned authority and institutional validity took charge. Suddenly, authority figures were looked upon with disdain. In fact, all levels of authority were under siege. The disrespect of the 1960s is still alive and well, and if there is any doubt, just become a college professor, doctor, policeman (among others), or even the President of the United States. Civility is only a memory.

To illustrate, I was teaching a graduate management course in the early 1990s as an academic sharecropper, when a student disagreed with what I was teaching. I was lecturing on the evolution of management thought and the role Frederick Winslow Taylor played in the consulting world at the turn of the 20th century. Well, the disgruntled student, in front of the class, challenged me, so I asked him to tell me specifically how I was wrong. He said he couldn't, but he didn't agree with my characterization of Taylor. After I failed to elicit an appropriate response from him, I left the lectern and sat down in a chair near the front of the classroom and told him to teach the rest of the class. He became indignant and refused to leave his seat, and I told him, "You're the expert, come on up and teach the class. Obviously, I don't know what I'm talking about, but you do, so come on up, because I'm ready to learn." He wouldn't take over so I had to resume, but he got the message that a little respect was in order, especially from a man like him who was wearing the uniform of his country.

Though it shouldn't surprise me, it always does when a student calls me *Mr.* Fountain or by my first name. I *earned* my doctorate in business administration D.B.A., and out of respect a student should address me as Dr. Fountain. I suppose the lack of respect shouldn't bother me, but it does. Hopefully, this expectation is not jaded by my southern upbringing where we were taught to be respectful to all—especially the elderly and women. We always said Mr. and Ma'am when we addressed a man or a woman. To this day, when I'm in the presence of one of my professors from the past, and some of them from long ago, I still refer to them as Dr. A short time back, I was doing business in a credit union branch and happened upon one of my old bosses from the days when I worked for the Department of Defense, and I referred to him as Mr. I worked for him for three years as his assistant and he tried to get me to call him by his first name then, but I had too much respect for him to do that. The point I'm making is cultural change should not result in a general lack of respect and civility. And, some of the changes which came out of the 1960s certainly contribute to a casualness of decorum that leads to the perception of disrespect. One of those changes was the introduction of the Student Faculty Evaluation.

STUDENT FACULTY EVALUATIONS

Questions of purpose and efficacy have swirled around the use of student faculty evaluations from the beginning. Initially, they were self-administered evaluations which professors held in confidence for the purpose of improving their approach to the courses they taught, but over time, this measurement device has evolved into a tool for administrators—a way of justifying decisions. A lot rides on getting good evaluations. Everything from promotions to tenure to retention to pay increases is determined, in large measure, from student evaluations. In the case of us academic sharecroppers, student faculty evaluations *rule*, because we are expendable. Since there are so many of us, and administrators have so little respect for us field hands, and because they have no allegiance when it comes to adjuncts, it's usually easy to get a new, academic sharecropper. What I would like to see is an anonymous academic sharecropper evaluation form which evaluates the administrators and support staff, but that will never happen because these people are too insecure and afraid of the truth.

I remember when I first began traveling down the adjunct faculty road and how proud I was to be associated with a number of universities for which I worked. I almost always got outstanding student evaluations and, at least on a conscious level, I never thought I compromised my integrity; although, the student evaluation was usually in the back of my mind. As I look back today, I believe that there were times I should have been more direct with students, rather than soft-peddling some of my rebuttals and responses when students were really out of line. But, I didn't want to appear to be difficult.

PURPOSE AND EFFICACY:

Though administrators downplay the significance and the purpose of student evaluations, they have a powerful effect on the future of a full-time faculty member or an academic sharecropper. Dr. Mark Shapiro has stated it quite well, "On the whole . . . student evaluations of teaching do not measure learning in any significant way. Instead, they measure student 'satisfaction' with the instructor and with other aspects of the course" (Shapiro – 3). That's part of the problem, and that raises the question, who's in charge? Anytime leadership lines are blurred and authority is compromised, role confusion is a natural outgrowth.

One of Dr. Shapiro's colleagues, Professor Michael Birnbaum, conducted a faculty survey about student evaluations that was quite telling, and in the words of Dr. Shapiro, ". . .72.1% of the faculty respondents felt that the use of student evaluations encourage faculty to 'water down' the content in their courses, while only 26.9% felt that this was not true" (Shapiro -2). In another survey, ". . . 38 percent of professors admitted to dumbing down their courses to get better evaluations . . . And in one study 70 percent of students admitted that their evaluation was influenced by the grade they expected to get" (Huemer 1). Dr. Paul Trout of Montana State University sees the "watering down" or "dumbed-down education," as he puts it, to be of concern as well, "For me, the key indictment against using numerical forms to reward and punish the classroom behavior of instructors is that it encourages instructors to dumb down their teaching . . . . If it takes consistently high evaluation scores to get raises, tenure, promotion and other perks, many instructors—consciously or unconsciously—will do what it takes to get those scores" (Trout 2-3). However, in the case of academic sharecroppers the only thing they can hope for is another contract for another course.

In an article which appeared in the *Washington Post,* Professor Trout addressed the lack of rigor for which professors are responsible as a result of student evaluations. He asked the question, "What makes many students happy nowadays? 'Understanding' and 'friendly' instructors, 'comfortable' courses and 'fair' grades. To translate: teachers who are not demanding, workloads that are not taxing and grading standards that are not high" (Trout 1).

Obviously, students are aware of the power of the evaluation. Many of them choose that opportunity to "get even." It is their way of venting anonymously. I have held positions in the education industry both as a full-time professor/ administrator and an academic sharecropper in which one of my responsibilities was to review student evaluations of the professors' performances. I could usually tell when a student was attempting to "nail" a professor, because I often checked with the professor and inquired about certain student comments, and most of the time the professor could connect the comment with something that happened in the class or something that had absolutely nothing to do with the course or quality of education. More often than not, the negative comments were related to the professor's personality, appearance, philosophy, or political persuasion.

INAPPROPRIATE FACTORS WHICH EFFECT STUDENT EVALUATIONS:

Whimsical factors such as attractiveness of the professor, wardrobe, grade expected, and enthusiastic tone of voice of the professor serves as influencers in the evaluation process. For example:

> *Daniel Hamermesh, a professor of economics at the University of Texas at Austin, and Amy Parker, one of his students, found that attractive professors consistently outscore their less comely colleagues by a significant margin on student evaluations of teaching . . . . Anyone who thinks looks don't count in academe is foolish says Judith Waters, a psychology professor at Fairleigh Dickinson University who studies the relationship of physical beauty to aging, income, and work. . . . [Hamermesh and Parker] also found that both female and minority professors earned lower overall ratings for their teaching than their white, male peers (Montell 1-2).*

According to Jean Wilson, WICB Committee, Assistant professor, Department of Cell Biology and Anatomy at the University of Arizona, there is gender bias in the student evaluation process. Males tend to rate female professors lower and male professors are unaffected by a student's gender (*Women in Cell Biology* 1).

Wardrobe as an influencer in the evaluation process is an interesting nuance. I can remember how some of my teachers dressed when I was in college, and I must admit sandals and worn jeans did not appeal to me, but I was more focused on the individual course and the quality of instruction, so the way they dressed, ponytails, and beards really didn't affect me. I judged the course based on what I thought I got out of it.

One time I was in Iowa teaching an MBA course. When I teach as an academic sharecropper, unlike most of my academic sharecropper colleagues, I dress in a coat and tie or a business suit. To me, that is the uniform of the day. I'm a business consultant and corporate trainer, and those of us in the consulting role dress in the appropriate attire. I taught my first class on a Friday evening. Saturday morning I came in to teach a four-hour session that lasted until noon. After I had called for a short break around 10:00 A.M., one of my male students approached me and commented, "Dr. Fountain, you really don't have to dress up for us, you can relax." In a good spirit I told him, "I'm not dressing up for you, I'm dressing up for me, and this is how I dress when I work. You folks are not on your jobs, but I am, and I don't expect you to dress formally. When Monday morning comes, and you report in to work, does your boss expect you to dress in a coat and tie?" He replied, "Absolutely." I sincerely thanked him for his concern, but I believe I made my point, because none of them mentioned it again. It's almost comical, because I frequently see comments about how spiffy I dress on student evaluation forms, as if that has anything to do with the course I'm teaching.

What role does enthusiasm play in the evaluation process? From my personal experience, it is an important influencer. I know that because I'm usually very upbeat and excited about teaching, and that is reflected in my student evaluations, but just how important is that? I have had many good professors who were there to give you their knowledge, and some of them did it in a very effective but dry way. For me, if I must make a choice, I prefer a professor who is sincere, competent, and can impart knowledge which I can integrate into my thinking, rather than a phony, motivational speaker who has little substance.

There was a study at Cornell University which drove home the point of just how important enthusiasm is when it comes to getting high ratings on the student faculty evaluation form. A professor at Cornell taught the identical course twice—once in the first-semester and then again in the second-semester. The first-semester he used less enthusiasm in his approach. When the second-semester came around, he showed more enthusiasm in tone of voice, and his ratings soared in every measure, i.e., such things as fairness in grading, the quality of the text, professor accessibility, etc., all went up. "And although the 249 students in the second-semester course said they learned more than the 229 students the previous semester believed they had learned, the two groups performed no differently on exams and other assessment measures" (Cornell University 1). This clearly demonstrates how style often is viewed as more important than substance. The Presidential Debates of 2004 are a poignant example. Nearly all of the media pundants said that Senator John F. Kerry won all three of the debates because of style, but that didn't prevent President George W. Bush from winning the election because of substance.

Research has even shown that whether or not a class is required rather than an elective has an effect on student evaluations, including the level of the student, that is, freshman, sophomore, junior, or senior. ". . . the more students in a class taking the course as a requirement the lower the overall rating will be. Moreover, freshmen tend to rate their teachers significantly lower than do sophomores; sophomores tend to rate them significantly lower than do juniors, and so on" (Emery, et al. 2).

REFLECTIONS ON THE EVOLUTION OF STUDENT EVALUATIONS

In 1973 only about 30 percent of U.S. colleges and universities were allowing students to evaluate professors, but now it's hard to find an educational institution that doesn't use student evaluations. Moreover, this practice has circled the globe. Since the 1960s there have been nearly 2000 studies conducted in higher education regarding this issue. It has become the most researched topic in higher education (Wilson 3).

Since students started this evaluation system in the 1960s, who is in charge and how reliable and valid are student evaluations of faculty (SEF)? It appears that from a reliability position, that the SEF system seems to measure what it was intended to measure, although there is some doubt about that, but validity is another issue. There is *not* a lot of evidence which suggests that positive correlation exists related to other measures of teaching effectiveness. It seems as though because the higher education industry has used this tool for so long that somehow it must be reliable and valid, which simply shouldn't be the case.

The problem seems to be that the use of SEF has become institutionalized, but that doesn't make its use reliable or valid—only accepted and practiced. Perhaps, the underlying issue is that most colleges and universities have become so customer oriented that they now are afraid to disappoint the "customer." In some ways, rightfully so, because from my experience, students nearly always get their way as soon as administrators become involved—which causes one to wonder, who is in charge?

Despite that, there is simply too much evidence which invalidates the SEF method to be continued. Study after study has shown that many types of student biases influence student responses on SEF forms.

What about the Dr. Fox Effect? There was a well known study conducted more than 30 years ago in which:

> . . . *a professional actor was hired to deliver a non-substantive and contradictory lecture, but in an enthusiastic and authoritative style. The audience, consisting of professional educators, had been told they would be listening to Dr. Myron Fox, an expert on the application of mathematics to human behavior. They were then asked to rate the lecture. Dr. Fox received highly positive ratings, and no one saw through the hoax* (Student Evaluations: A Critical Review 3).

In addition, there have been a number of other studies which have shown the fallacy of such evaluation systems. It seems obvious that too much emphasis is placed on the value of such evaluation techniques. Further, I think T.L. Simmons said it well in his article "Student Evaluation of Teachers: Professional Practice or Punitive Policy?" Simmons summed it up as follows:

> *Student evaluations of teacher effectiveness (SETEs) are, at best, nothing more than evaluations of the students' perceptions of the teachers' effectiveness. . . . It should be intuitively apparent to most that opinions expressed are subject to a great many variables that may have little or nothing to do with evaluating the teachers' ability to teach* (Simmons 2).

Although there are many well respected administrators such as Jack Daniel, Vice Provost for Academic Affairs, of the University of Pittsburgh who believes that, "The system in place does work" (*University Times* 1), I must respectfully disagree. Any system which is so flawed should be discarded if it is used for the purposes of academic sharecropper retention and other personnel decisions affecting the futures of full-time faculty members. It would seem to me that peer review and greater involvement on the part of administrators in evaluating and assessing performance of professors should take precedence over student opinion. After all, why are students sitting in the classroom? If they know so much about what quality education is and is not, why aren't they teaching the course? Professor Larry Crumbley of Louisiana State University said it well:

> *Complaints are often voiced that students are not qualified to evaluate many areas of instructor effectiveness. A senior in high school is not qualified to evaluate high school teachers, yet 4 or 5 months later this same freshman in college has developed the maturity and judgment to evaluate higher education* (Crumbley 5).

In the normal business world who evaluates the performance of his or her workers? Usually, it is the supervisor or manager of that employee, unless the organization has employed a 360 degree performance appraisal system. Then, peers, other managers above and below, and those outside the department or organization participate in the overall assessment of the employee, along with the immediate supervisor.

Finally, it is not my position to argue for the elimination of student input, but rather to place their input into proper perspective. They are not the experts, we are. As I see it, the student faculty evaluations have become tools used to exploit the system. They were never intended for the purposes for which they are being used—now they are little more than implements used to exploit the higher education industry. What we have is the tail wagging the dog.

Chapter Eight

Administrative Incompetence—Strategic Bungling

NE WOULD THINK THAT THOSE OCCUPYING positions in the higher education industry would be paragons of administrative competence and strategic thinking, but that is hardly the case. As Paul Trummel, webspinner@ContraCabal.org, has explained bureaucratic bungling in one of his apropos articles:

> *Powerful, non-educating, absolutist university officials and powerless faculty and student bodies have become one of the most elemental problems facing contemporary higher learning. Consequently, the politically motivated, administrative power structure now interferes with the pedagogic process. Crucially, any improvement must accompany significant changes in the structure and employment of those who wield power.*

It's ironic, because just as I titled this chapter, while sitting at my computer on October 21, 2004, I received an e-mail from an educational institution, I *think* offering me a contract to teach a doctoral course in a different city from whence I hail. I say I *think*, because the e-mail was only a recommendation that I teach the course, not a contract. This wouldn't be too bad if it weren't for the fact that the course is scheduled to begin in less than three months. This is not a survey course at a community college where preparation time is minimized, it is a *doctoral* course. Hopefully, within the next couple of weeks, I'll know if I need to become a freeway flyer again in January. The only reason that I'll accept this assignment, if it comes through, is because I only have to teach this class for a total of three weekends over a three-month period and, in my experience, I will be receiving premium pay in the gross amount of $6,000, that is, if there are at least 14 students in the class; otherwise, my pay goes down. I suppose that's not too bad, because if there are just 14 students, the university will only gross a mere $42,000, but if there are more than 14 students in the class, the university's gross goes up, but my compensation remains the same. After my pay and expenses, the university should net about $32,000. After taxes, my net will be about $4,000. As I see it, the university will receive approximately eight times that which I will. But, as an academic sharecropper, who thoroughly enjoys teaching, what more should I expect?

The administrative incompetence and strategic bungling I speak of confounds most who know the details of my experiences with the higher education industry. There are so many mind boggling scenarios to share that even I have difficulty in accepting the numerous examples, but the following will serve well in establishing the administrative and strategic bungling of a number of institutions of higher learning.

SCENARIO ONE:

A number of years ago, I was lured away from a Fortune 500 company to build a new entrepreneurial, educational venture for a university. The chairman of the board of trustees liked me and my interest in teaching, so he encouraged me to join the university as a full-time faculty member and administrator. I wanted to do it, but I didn't like having to take a $10,000 pay cut, so the president and the vice president of academic affairs assured me that if I made the new program a success, they would make sure I was rewarded accordingly.

In less than a year I collected more than $50,000 from students who wanted to be in the new program. The new venture was an overwhelming success. Even one of the more influential members of the board of trustees couldn't believe that the venture had been so successful. But, I worked hard doing something I truly loved. All went well until the new faculty contracts came out the next year. I reviewed my contract and found that I had only received a three percent increase. I found out later that was what all the other faculty members had received. But, at the time, I thought for sure there had to be a mistake, so I made an appointment with the vice president of academic affairs. The next morning I went to see him, and I told him about our previous agreement. Unfortunately, he had fallen victim to amnesia, because he couldn't remember ever telling me that I would be rewarded separately from the regular faculty. As he sat at his desk looking up at me as I stood, he said, "Wendell, I don't recall ever making that kind of promise. I can't give you a different percentage than the regular faculty, there'll be a mutiny."

I left quite disappointed, because I realized at that moment that these people were not honorable and were administrative and strategic incompetents. It affected me quite deeply, because it took the wind out of my sails that I so desperately needed. Until then, I had felt as though I was on top of the world. As I was returning to my office across the campus, I thought about all the occasions I had gotten free television and radio time to promote the program. I had practically begged a features writer at the newspaper to do a story about us, she did, and it worked. We tracked the number of students who enrolled in our program over the following six months, and because of that one article, we discovered that we added an additional 69 students.

I had to get as much free publicity as possible, because the university only gave me a pittance for marketing and advertising. The comptroller, who controlled the purse strings, was a retired U.S. Navy admiral and didn't have a clue about what he was doing. Of course, that would have been true of a heart surgeon or anyone else who was not trained in finance. Quite often, I and the admiral had shouting matches about my budget shortfalls that he created without my input. There is a simple lesson here. Don't hire people because of their past fame or position in life unless they possess the necessary skills to do the job.

Though I had brought new money into the university and members of the administration gave me public affirmation, behind the scenes they refused to give me the resources I needed to maintain the level of progress I had sustained. Once they got the new money, they wouldn't reinvest enough of it to make a significant difference. The reason is simple; it's called administrative incompetence and strategic bungling. After agonizing with this mess for some time, a couple of years later I quit in disgust and began devoting full time to my business, which in retrospect I should have done a lot earlier, because I would have been much farther ahead of the game if I had.

SCENARIO TWO:

Once I did a four-year stint, as an academic sharecropper ($2,500 per course), for a university located in the Midwest which I considered to be a reputable institution. It was accredited and internationally recognized and had satellite campuses in the U.S. and abroad. I taught many graduate courses for them on military bases before I'd had enough.

The problems which perplexed me most were with the satellite administrator. We had a very strained relationship from the beginning because of certain operational issues—like the assignment of grades. At the end of each term I was always faced with completion of the grade sheet within a five-day period, which I was always able to do until my last course, because she and her staff always insisted that I sign the grade sheet and then call in the grades to the university office, and they would write in the grade. That never settled well with me, and I avoided doing as they wanted by getting the grades in within the time frame they required. The last course I taught ended in an angry exchange between me and the site administrator. That was the first time it was going to take me longer to complete the grading process than normal, and she insisted that I come in and sign the grade sheet so that they could record the grades when I called the office. I objected strenuously, because I told her that was an unethical expectation and practice, and that I had no way of knowing that the grade I called in was being recorded appropriately. She took exception to my comment, but I didn't care, because I was not about to cooperate in an unethical practice. Moreover, I didn't trust her, because she seemed more interested in adding and retaining students than ensuring that the quality of education was maintained. I had observed her and taught many of the students, and many of them were marginally qualified at best.

Though I had some reservations about the campus administrators, I was reluctant to indict the entire university, but it was hard for me to believe that someone at the top had no knowledge of what this woman was doing. She obviously received recognition for the dollars she was responsible for bringing into the campus coffers. In addition, she expanded the program in that location greatly, and that had to have pleased the administration.

SCENARIO THREE:

I have saved this one for last, because it is surely the *coup de grâce*. I fought hard to keep this bunch of administrative incompetents from injuring themselves and the historic educational institution for which we worked, but in the end they accomplished just what they intended, the adoption of a retrenchment strategy which left them financially strapped. They of course were full-time employees, and I was only an academic sharecropper and business consultant. As part of their retrenchment strategy, they closed sites in Florida and Puerto Rico which made absolutely no business sense.

After warning them for two years that they needed to do some marketing in Florida, they finally accepted my marketing proposal in my role as a business consultant, not as an academic sharecropper. I had worked in that role (adjunct), among others, for them for the better part of 20 years. Six weeks after my six-month contract started, they told me they had decided to close two key sites in Florida. I was shocked by the news, because by then I and my associate had already made significant inroads in Florida during the six weeks of the contract. We had gotten the ball rolling at a fever pace. I couldn't believe that such a foolish decision had been made, so I tried to plead with them—but to no avail.

Ultimately, these incompetents ended up turning down two outstanding opportunities that would have brought them in nearly $1,000,000 in two years at minimal costs. One of the opportunities I brought them was a deal with the University Partnership Center located in St. Petersburg, Florida, but they turned that down, too, despite the fact that all they would have had to pay the Center was a mere $500 per course sponsored by the university I represented. The classes would have been held in a new, state of the art teaching facility where an additional

12 universities were partners comprised of such institutions as the University of Florida, Florida State University, University of Central Florida, and George Washington University. Even more amazing, the Center spent $200,000 annually on advertising for the university partners, which didn't cost the partners a dime. Even though the university turned everything down, they still paid me nearly $10,000 for my efforts. Why I don't know, because they refused everything I brought them. I know this sounds like a fictional yarn, but please keep in mind this is a nonfiction book. Everything written is an accurate account of what went on at this institution.

This has to be one of the worst run educational institutions I've ever seen—from the chairman of the board, who doesn't answer your letters, to the lowest level administrator. Like so many institutions of higher learning, it really is likened to just moving the deck chairs around on the Titanic, because one day a person would be a director and the next an associate dean or the other way around. On occasion they would get rid of someone if it was politically expedient; otherwise, they just recycled the inept, as power, politics, and pettiness propelled them around the campus. In the end, after nearly 20 years of serving this institution, these Inspector Cleauseau types jettisoned me, because they became tired of having their feet held to the fire.

WHAT HAPPENS WHEN POWER, POLITICS, AND PETTINESS CONVERGE?

The answer to that question is quite simple, because a massive, academic bloodletting occurs in which good people get hurt. I could share many anecdotes which I have observed during my sharecropping days, but I'll limit it to just one to make my point. Central to this problem is fundamental administrative incompetence borne out of envy, jealousy, and insecurity. There's one institution with which I've had a long-term relationship where I've seen many fine faculty members and administrators in various colleges suffer the flings and arrows of disgruntled, nefarious department chairs, deans, and directors all because of the three P's—power, politics, and pettiness (PPP).

This account is centered on a female administrator whom I've known for more than 20 years. Though we never really became close friends, she was someone I liked and admired a great deal. I watched her work at a distance and she was very innovative, creative, and highly competent. She proposed a business opportunity to the dean of the college of business, but he shied away from it and chose to pass. At that point she was working under the dean's leadership, but she was so confident that the new graduate program she envisioned would be a success; she took the idea to a different college in the university that choose to implement the new program and to let her head it up.

Over nearly four years her new program grew like wildfire, and she became the envy of just about everyone. She brought in millions of new dollars into the university. Of course, becoming high profile can be risky, because there's almost always someone taking aim from behind a bush or tree with the hope of knocking you out of the saddle. To this day, I still don't know for sure who was responsible for her undoing, but she not only left the job, but ended up leaving the university. After she departed, pure chaos ensued. I know, because I was working under her direction as a sharecropper when these events went down. Then, the parade of new deans and administrators began. There were three changes in the top leadership position in less than a year. No one knew who was on first, second, third, or for that matter, no one even knew if there was a game in play. It almost became a joke, but it wasn't funny, because I never knew who to call about what. Moreover, I saw other good people sacrificed on the PPP alter. Some of whom also had to leave the university. The last time I dealt with this organization, the only thing different was things had gotten even worse.

FACULTY DEVELOPMENT MEETINGS (FDMs)

Every time I have attended faculty development meetings for these various universities for which I sharecropped, I usually left the meetings aggravated, frustrated, and confused, because none of those meetings were ever really about development. They were not about listening to you or your concerns, e.g., one incident readily comes to mind that makes the point. For three years in a row I attended an annual FDM in which I and a colleague brought up a need to make a fundamental change in the student guide for graduate students completing their major projects, but nothing was ever done, and I seriously doubt it has been addressed to this day. Most of the time, the meetings focused on what we academic sharecroppers were doing wrong and what the university expected us to do about it. Sometimes, FDMs were only an information sharing vehicle, that is, an opportunity to tell you how procedures had changed and what you had to do to accommodate those changes, which usually resulted in more work and no more money.

Listening to and watching these incompetent, administrative careerists perform was a chore. I wouldn't think that way if there had been more substance and less posturing by administrators. Usually, these meetings were held at some distant location which required you to drive or fly, and I might add, for no compensation. More often than not, we sharecroppers gave up a weekend to attend those gatherings.

One of the things which usually came out of these FDMs was that administrators would shove off more of their duties and responsibilities on us without additional pay or for some insulting amount like being paid $25.00 per hour to conduct academic advising for the university, while they sat back on the campus making six-figure salaries. There always seemed to be no end to the opportunities to exploit the academic sharecropper.

ADMINISTRATIVE INCOMPETENCE—A GENERALIZED PROBLEM

Looking back on my career in the higher education industry, it is easy to see what is wrong with the industry, and essentially, it's self-perpetuating and self-serving. My experiences could just be written off as coincidence, that I only worked for a bunch of loser schools, led by packs of bureaucratic, incompetent administrators, but I submit that the problem is far greater. As Dennis Redovich of the Center for the Study of Jobs & Education in Wisconsin said, "It is unbelievable how university top administrators, like corporate CEOs have convinced their governing boards that they are primarily responsible for all of the accomplishments of the organization and are indispensable" (Redovich 2).

The first issue to examine is the concept of "incompetence." What does it actually mean and how is it identified? According to David A. Dunning, professor of psychology at Cornell University, and Justin Kruger, assistant professor at the University of Illinois, an incompetent person may not know they are incompetent. "People who do things badly are usually supremely confident of their abilities—more confident, in fact, than people who do things well . . . . skills required for competence often are the same skills necessary to recognize incompetence" (Goode 1). Professor Kruger wrote, "Not only do they reach erroneous conclusions and make unfortunate choices, but their incompetence robs them of the ability to realize it." Perhaps, this explains why so many administrators in education with whom I have had working relationships have demonstrated incompetent decision making in an inexplicable manner accompanied by anomalies of behavior.

ADMINISTRATIVE INCOMPETENCE AT THE NATIONAL LEVEL

There are many examples across the U.S. of gross incompetence at institutions of higher education. West Virginia University had its problems back in 1995. President David C. Hardesty, Jr. found the following problems to be unsolved.

❖ <u>The abandonment of *in locus parentis* had been taken too far</u> – alcohol abuse was a problem and alternatives hadn't been offered the students.

❖ <u>There was a dangerous back-to-school block party every year</u> - crowds had become too much for the local police, and two people were injured by gunfire the previous year.

❖ <u>The lack of respect was evident on campus</u> – dangerous behavior at sporting events had been observed and residence halls had been vandalized.

❖ <u>The lack of respect was a two-way street</u> – students were standing in line for 4-6 hours to register for class, or finally reaching the end of the line only to be told that the office was closing business for the day.

❖ <u>Enrollment was dropping</u>.

❖ <u>Town-grown relationships were strained</u>.

Fortunately, President Hardesty showed administrative competence and leadership skills by taking control of the situation. Over the next five years he turned things around, and that was good for the university and all concerned, but the issue is where were the administrators of that institution?

What were they doing? How did they let things get that far? The answer is simple—incompetence, because this situation did not develop over night.

Another example is the University of Texas where Brian Leiter reported that after repeated attempts to get the administration to correct errors and omissions in a web page devoted to "listing the honors accrued by the faculty," the corrections fell on deaf ears. The page listed three recently deceased outstanding scholars rather than living, outstanding members of the faculty. Moreover, another page listed James A. Baker, former Secretary of State, as a faculty member, but Leiter could only speculate that at sometime in the past James A. Baker might have served as an adjunct, since he was a UT alum, but he certainly was not a current faculty member. As Leiter explained it, "None of this has any intrinsic interest or significance obviously. But it makes one marvel at the peculiar pace at which bureaucratic structures operate. . . . I am sure Max Weber must have the answer" (Leiter, Brian 1-2). I agree with Brian Leiter about the importance of this issue, but it is indicative of the hebetudes of bureaucratic bungling; however, there are issues of a greater concern about which everyone in the U.S. has an interest—terrorism.

April 8, 2002, an article appeared in *Issues & Views* warning that immigration fraud is rampant, and universities are at the centerpiece of opportunity. Greedy leaders and administrators of some of America's most elite colleges and universities are more concerned about the financial impact that immigration laws will have on their institutions than the safety of the nation. They are against any fiat associated with changing student visas, because that might limit the number of profitable, foreign students they can attract. "For example, Boston University now has 5,240 foreign students, researchers or professors. . . . At least 40 percent of foreign students in the United States currently receive financial aid, and major colleges recently announced that they will substantially increase aid to foreign students" (*Issues & Views* 1). Obviously, most foreign students, researchers, and professors abhor acts of terrorism as much as any American, but every possible entry point into this country must be carefully scrutinized. We know how some of the terrorists of September 11, 2001 got into this country, and we know that the first plane that hit the twin towers was piloted by the terrorist Mohammed Atta. He and other murdering terrorists used the educational industry to enable them to carry out the horrific act perpetrated on 3,000 innocent human beings by destroying the twin towers of the World Trade Center.

We know for a fact institutions such as Embry-Riddle Aeronautical University and Huffman Aviation International Flight School in Venice, Florida were used in teaching the terrorists how to fly airplanes. We also know for a fact that Sami Al-Arian, once a professor at the University of South Florida, was associated with terror organizations and a terror cell in Tampa, Florida, and now he sits in a prison cell. It's only logical and responsible for the leaders of the United States to enact laws, rules, and regulations which help us to minimize terror, with the exception of some university administrators who can only see dollar signs.

Only a few weeks after the terrorists' attack of September 11, 2001, an administrator at Central Michigan University had the unmitigated gall to insist that students take down their patriotic posters, because the posters might offend someone. Foolish administrators shut down a website at Duke University after Professor Gary Hull posted an article which called for a military response to the terrorist attack—so much for free speech. Finally, The Dean of Library services at Florida Gulf Coast University had her employees remove stickers proclaiming "Proud to be an American," because it could be offensive to international students—how stupid! I think the murder of 3,000 innocent Americans by a bunch of barbarians has more significance than some international student's sensitivity (*Issues & Views* 1-2). If this type of idiotic thinking had existed during World War II, Americans or whatever we would be called would be speaking either German or Japanese today.

Administrative bungling involves many areas of endeavor. Philip Ross, writing for *The Tower Online* of Catholic University of America, has concern about the stifling of debate by administrators at his institution. Ross was disturbed that D.C. Delegate Eleanor Holmes Norton "has been uninvited from signing copies of her recently released book." His position is that it is absurd to create such an embarrassing image bursting situation, because universities should be a place where debate is welcomed, not censored. Ross described the administration's modus operandi as, "The common formula here is: an invitation or award offer is extended, some student group or administrator gets offended, University rescinds offer and CUA receives negative press," He added, "My question is, why does this administrative bungling continue to be tolerated?" (Ross 1). His question is a good one, and the answer is obvious—incompetence. It is because of a general lack of quality leadership.

Even Harvard University has been accused by the government of bungling a critical Russian government-funded mission to Moscow back in the 1990s. In September of 2000 the U.S. Attorney in Boston sued Harvard and four defendants for playing investment games which were in conflict with the existing contract. "Whereupon the U.S. government accused Harvard of failing to monitor the project properly, demanding $120 million in damages, or three times the value of the $34 million contract" (economicprincipals.com).

The suit was aimed at Professor Andrei Shleifer, a distinguished Harvard economist, his deputy, lawyer Jonathan Hay, Shleifer's wife Nancy Zimmerman, and Hay's companion, Elizabeth Hebert. In addition, the President of Harvard, Lawrence Summers, who was mentored by professor Shleifer when he was a junior economist at the university, has told the faculty to keep Shleifer on board.

Pace University seems to have difficulty in ensuring that the printing company, E-Pro, it uses for the publication, *The Pace Press,* gets paid for the University's printing services. "Student Development and Campus Activities allocates a budget to the Press and approves every cent we spend. But, ladies and gents, SDACA reports to Accounts Payable before we can have access to our cash. . . . The Press is trapped deep within the gaseous bowels of the University bureaucracy." The paper also reported that on occasion editors have actually had to pay for the printing out of pocket or on credit cards and then wait months to get reimbursed (*The Pace Press* 1-2). This is pure and simple, ineptness.

In an article by Anthony Dick, *Cavalier Daily* Columnist, he reported that a mother had created a Web site which called for the University of Virginia to get out of the business of trying to handle cases of sexual assault. The mother charged that the University had turned a blind eye to the situation after her daughter was raped by a fellow student. "Sexual assault is much too serious an offense to be handled through a process under the watch of bungling University administrators. . . . Rapists shouldn't just be kicked out of the University. They should be locked up in prison" (Dick, 1-3).

Professor M. Millman of the College Math Department of LaGuardia Community College has written a series of scathing memos accusing the administration under which he works of gross incompetence. In one memo, regarding invasion of privacy, he slammed the administration for allowing names of faculty members to show on copies of student evaluations that another professor had procured from the Personnel Department. He proclaimed, "Even by LaGuardia standards, this is mind-boggling incompetence of epic proportions" (Millman Memo dated 11/14/00). In another memo he charged that the administration was guilty of political cronyism. "This kind of unethical politicking inevitably allows crony faculty, having the barest qualifications and the worst student ratings, to secure tenure, promotions, and leadership positions solely on the basis of their political affiliation (Millman Memo dated 5/17/00. Professor Millman has written extensively about the failures of his administration, the two cited above are among many in which he has been very critical of his leadership.

In summary, administrative incompetence and strategic bungling are manifold in higher education. There seems to be an endless stream of examples. It's reasonable to conclude that my specific examples presented earlier in this chapter are broadly applicable to the higher education industry, and that fundamental incompetence exists in places where one would not expect to find it.

Chapter Nine

Student Customer—Customer Student

*I*F AN EDUCATIONAL INSTITUTION UNDERSTANDS this dichotomy and philosophically responds appropriately, the quality of education does not suffer as much as it might. The title of this chapter is more than a play on words; it has substantive meaning which has tremendous influence on an institution's approach to education. When students are viewed as customers first rather than second, the quality of education is compromised, because students are products of education. "Students are not our customers—they are our products. We need to improve students' value by educating them. Society and employers are our customers" (Crumbley 7). The tendency for even the best of colleges and universities to become diploma mills increases when students are considered to be customers. Any and all educational institutions should attend to deficiencies in the systems which are responsible for the delivery of educational services, but when it comes to the actual educational experience, the student should no longer be thought of as a customer. A student should not be able to exert inordinate influence on professors who are crucial to the provision of the educational service. The creation of a customer service model in which the student is led to believe that the professor is an employee of the student is a mistake.

One can liken this to the patient-physician relationship. I am a professional business consultant and educator, I am not a physician, though I know I am paying for medical services and employing the person, I am not their boss, it is not my place to tell the physician how to do his or her job. They have been educated and trained in a highly specialized field and are my paid resource for maintaining or improving my health.

I have had a number of physicians return to college and take graduate business courses which I have taught, because they knew I was the professional in business and they were not, and I might add, I was always treated as the professional by everyone of them. That's why I take exception to students who want to treat me as their employee, and if the model that the university embraces is one of customer-student approach rather than student-customer, problems generally arise. The entire issue around a customer service approach tends to commoditize and marginalize the unique educational experience. Getting an education is not like someone providing plumbing services or repairing one's car. From my experience, universities who view students as customers first are those institutions given to the highest degree of exploitation of faculty of all types, including academic sharecroppers like me, as well as the higher education industry in general. To those institutions the bottom line is the bottom line and business is business.

ORGANIZATIONAL CULTURE AFFECTATIONS

Student-customer thinking is affected by organizational factors. President, Dr. Shirley Raines, of the University of Memphis recognized that the students were not receiving accurate or timely information from the various functional offices of the University. Staff found it difficult and time consuming to disseminate accurate information outside their areas of expertise, and the students as well found it to be time consuming. So, she found an information technology solution for the problem called RightNow Service™ because, "Our students expected better from us. . . . It was essential that we find ways to utilize technology to provide faster services to our students and faculty" (RightNow Technologies 2). This was a good decision, and there's nothing wrong with improving these kinds of services, because that is exactly what should happen. The rub comes when this kind of thinking flows into matters of an academic nature—like student faculty evaluations.

Educational reforms of all types are having an effect on administrators and faculty regarding their perception of students. Organizational cultural morphing causes new and different ways of looking at the student. As changes occur, "The significance of organizational culture becomes particularly clear as we operationalize institutional transformation" (Lorenzen 1). Others have argued that organizational structures which have not factored in the information and technology-age are out of sync. One view espoused by Terry Obanion is that . . . "to serve an information-age society, we need to transform educational organizations by requiring teachers to design and manage, not deliver, customized learning experiences that include many options, including stand-alone technology and opportunities to learn outside of school" (Morrison 1). It is without doubt that the higher education industry is evolving at a rapid rate, and evolution is normal and expected. Time has never stood still for any business or industry—things change. What's important is how change is integrated into educational reform. If an organization culture fully emerges within the higher education industry which will not relinquish the position of the student-customer focus, then I for one am glad to be departing from higher education. It's unseemly for professors to continue to patronize students at all levels of higher education while full-time faculty and academic sharecroppers play the role of employee of the student. Reform does not have to be feared or rejected, but it should be respected and accepted where applicable. For example, Total Quality Management (TQM) is one management philosophy which has some management techniques that have much to offer higher education.

THE TOTAL QUALITY MANAGEMENT *(TQM)* MOVEMENT

The influence of W. Edwards Deming regarding his 14 principles of Total Quality Management (TQM) has been felt by many institutions of higher education. The concept took a foothold in the mid-1980s when the business world readily accepted TQM (Student As Customers 1). Southern Polytechnic State University of Georgia has, "A five-year TQM . . . grant from IBM Corporation [which] encouraged change, some of which flowed from a continual improvement course taken by more than 80% of Southern Polytechnic's employees. . . . Today, there is a consensus on the student as primary customer" (Wallace 1). This is a fundamental error, because they are more than consumers of a service—they are the product which must undergo the conversion process of human knowledge development and growth.

I have always maintained a high level of respect for Dr. Deming's work in Japan and here in the U.S., but to assume that TQM is a one-size fits all "new Philosophy of management" (to quote Dr. Deming) is a misapplication of the TQM approach. In the early 1990s, I received a call from the Human Resource Office of the Naval Air Station in Jacksonville, Florida. The Director of HRO wanted me to speak with a commanding officer of one of the tenant commands for which HRO had responsibility about TQM. In my role as a business consultant and corporate trainer I happily complied.

In my meeting with the captain I asked him just how much he wanted me to tell military members and the civilians he had under his command about Dr. Deming's 14 points. He looked at me incredulously and said, "I want you to tell them the whole thing, you do introductions to TQM, don't you?" I nodded then added, "The reason I asked that question, sir, is because there are some things you need to be prepared to do if you are to fully accept Dr. Deming's TQM approach. Let me illustrate by asking you the following question, "Are you willing to throw out the military member fitness report system and the civilian performance evaluation system?" He looked at me wide-eyed and said, "Hell no, I can't do that! That's required by law!" Well, I knew regardless of what the Secretary of Navy had decreed; the U.S. Navy could only adopt certain TQM practices, because it had its limitations in the actual implementation phase. Needless to say, the captain said he would have to get back with me, but that never happened.

Now, the military knows what I knew then, TQM won't fully work in the military environment, because the military's mission is different from industry. The mission of the military is to protect, destroy, and break things. Industry's mission is to build and provide products and services that people need, want, or demand so that businesses can flourish. TQM won't fully work in the educational environment either, because students are more than customers, they are the results of education. They cannot be processed like a product in a manufacturing plant. "Hence university faculties impose language, science, mathematics, and other requirements on undergraduates, knowing full well that all of the immediate consumers or customers, the students, will not be happy campers" (Yudof 6). This underscores the fundamental difference between business and education. In a successful business it is imperative that the customer not only be satisfied but, if at all possible, delighted. And, we know that many of our students are not pleased and definitely not delighted with having to measure up to a legitimate, challenging educational standard.

THE DILEMMA

Obviously, there are many professional educators who reject this concept of student-customer or for that matter the customer-student model.

> *Over the past years there has been considerable discussion as to whether or not we should use the term customer when referring to our students. Those who feel we should not . . . believe it connotes a devaluing of the important, traditional inspirational and mentoring roles faculty play in the lives of their students. . . . We live at a time when the educational franchise has been seen as an entrepreneurial opportunity for exploitation* (Smith 1).

It is evident that the educational industry has evolved into a highly competitive business, at a market level, and colleges and universities are doing their best to attract students, but at what cost? The cost should not exceed the academic integrity of the institution. Should a mindset be created which causes students to regard the professor as their employee rather than the professional who has knowledge about the subject which the student doesn't? Of course not, when I was a student, I had great respect for the position which my professors held—even when a small number of them did not live up to my expectations. Is it possible to become a value-added institution without compromising educational integrity? Without question it is, and the worst which will happen is that such an educational institution will attract the best and the brightest—thereby elevating the level of respect for the institution internally and externally.

One example about which I've had personal experience as an academic sharecropper is Eckerd College's Program for Experienced Learners (PEL). The main campus is located in St. Petersburg, Florida, where I have found undergraduate students, in many instances, in PEL to be comparable to MBA students or, in some cases, even doctoral level students at other institutions. This private college has not yet succumbed to the commodity mentality. Eckerd values the educational experience above the need to have overflowing classes. That college prides itself in providing a small class environment, unlike so many institutions which are customer-student oriented with a market focus. Coincidentally, when I was developing the College of Weekend Studies at Jacksonville University in the mid-1980s I visited Eckerd College to learn about PEL. I used many of Eckerd's concepts in my model at Jacksonville University, never thinking that someday I would teach courses for that institution. I'm sure Eckerd College is not the only exception in the higher educational industry, but it certainly is in the minority, because most colleges and universities are bottom line driven and market focused.

Following the open enrollment strategy, let anyone in who would like to register, catering to the student at all costs, and pushing for numbers results in attracting the least qualified, while diluting the educational experience. That usually is achieved by pursuing a marketing strategy, i.e., view the student as a customer rather than a student. Any student who is enrolled in a college or university which views the student as a customer is nearly guaranteed a degree, because if a problem arises such as poor grades or lack of attendance, just complain to the appropriate administrator and all will be fine, regardless of what the professor thinks.

Some educators see value in a marketing strategy, but in a limited way, "The market analogy is fine for nonacademic functions, such as book purchases, food service, or parking, but not for academics. A university is different from a consumer business" (Laskey 1). I couldn't agree more with Laskey. Everything should not be reduced to a commodity as most things. Even a ticket on an airplane has become a commodity, and that is one of the reasons why service is almost nonexistent. Using commodity logic will only lessen the value of a degree.

Unlike Eckerd College, I have had other experiences with educational institutions which wanted every class to be bulging at the seams. In the mid-1990s I was asked by a southern university to go to the island of Jamaica and teach two sections of international business in the weekend MBA program. I had been traveling around the U.S. conducting corporate training for several months and this sounded almost like a series of mini vacations, because the course was to be taught on five weekends over a 10-week period during the months of July, August, and September. I was pleased about the opportunity to return to Jamaica. I had only been there once before and had enjoyed it very much.

Little did I know what I was about to face. Upon my arrival, I was driven down the coast to one of the super clubs of Jamaica where I would be staying each of the weekends of my classes. My initial reaction was very positive, because the citizens of Jamaica are very accommodating, pleasant, and helpful. The next morning a driver took me to my first class back down the coast and up on a hill overlooking the ocean, where I found 28 MBA students sweltering in a cramped classroom in a little round building. The little building had no air conditioning, and I was dressed in a light summer suit and tie. It didn't take me long to shed as much clothing as I could, because by 10:00 A.M. I was drenched in perspiration and so were the students, even though they had dressed for the hot temperature. We had a couple of light rain showers the first morning and the sun came right back out, and the building turned into a sauna. Thankfully, we did have one small fan and lots of water which gave us all a little relief. My class lasted until noon, and my driver came to pick me up to take me to the next site.

He took me up on a mountain where I met my other class at 1:00 P.M. I had hoped there would be air conditioning at this site—but there was not. I thought my first group was large for an MBA class, but this one dwarfed it. To my consternation, I had 45 students in the class. Fortunately, the room was larger, but that helped little, because hardly anyone could hear over two large fans which were on high speed. That was a long afternoon. We finished at 5:00 P.M., and I was drowning in my own perspiration. When my driver came and picked me up, I was ecstatic.

I went to my room at the super club and peeled off my soggy clothes. I got in the shower with nothing on but the cold water. I stayed in there for nearly 30 minutes while the water cooled me down. When I got out, I flopped on the bed and slept for an hour. When I awoke, I went shopping for clothes appropriate for the climate and teaching and then got some nourishment. This particular university could have told me what I was going to encounter, but being the greedy, selfish, exploitive, bunch that they are; they let me find it out on my own.

I had a total of 73 MBA students, paying tuition of $1,000 each in an international business class. When you run the numbers, the university grossed $73,000 (books not included) for the two classes before my pay, which was $2,000 for each class, which left them with a gross of $69,000. After my expenses, I estimate the university had a net of $63,000. The sad thing about the situation was the university didn't care about the students, because we had to use an old textbook which predated the tearing down of the wall in 1989, marking the end of the old Soviet Union. In order to make the class meaningful, I had to bring in a lot of supplemental information, so that the students could get the value for which their organizations paid. In this instance both the students and I were exploited beyond reason. When this outfit is contrasted to an Eckerd College, there is no comparison. That organization is a strong believer in the student as a customer concept. I swore I would never teach again for this institution in a place without air conditioning—and I didn't.

GREED—A MOTIVATOR

No matter whether or not it's university administrators exploiting sharecroppers like me or playing fast and loose with labor regulations, it's all about greed. Greedy administrators are comfortable with the student-customer model among other money making opportunities, because they can bring in more revenue.

As a society we have begun to accept rottenness regardless of which historic, honored practice or institution is affected. The public at large has become desensitized to the excesses either read or heard about on nearly a daily basis. We are used to corporate greed and the attendant trappings which go with opulence. Three years ago, I thought it was almost criminal for the Board of Directors of the Disney Corporation to give Michael Eisner, then Chairman *and* CEO of the company a ten year contract worth $700 million. To me, every board member who supported this ridiculous compensation should have been summarily bounced off the board. With all due respect to Mr. Eisner, neither he nor anyone is worth that kind of money. I doubt very seriously he needed the money because, since the mid-80s, he has cashed in $850 million of Disney stock. I believe I've had dozens of students in my classes over the years that could have run the company just as well as Mr. Eisner. It is highly unlikely that even a maniacal CEO bent on destruction of Disney could ruin the company, because the management team and Disney culture are so strong and focused that such a thing would be nearly impossible.

This tendency to overcompensate leaders and administrators has spilled over into the higher education industry to those who are not coaches in the various sports programs. According to Rau and Bell, the Chancellor's salary of Louisiana State University went from $100,000 in 1990 to $490,000 in 2002 along with $500,000 in annuities and investments, while professor salaries remained flat at about

$50,000 per year. Other professionals' salaries also remained relatively flat at about $30,000 per year, while custodial salaries rested at $13,500 (Rau & Bell 1-4). Let the exploitation of those who are responsible for delivery of the educational experience continue! What Rau and Bell did not disclose is the pathetic amount paid to academic sharecroppers. The amount would be less than what the custodial staff earns.

LABOR GAMES AND GREED:

Exploitive administrators, because of their personal greed, find ways to make themselves look good by taking advantage of others. "Casual workers" at UCLA work 364 days per year and are fired and then rehired after the 365th day. It's a slick, nefarious way of playing games with labor laws. Some of these employees have worked for the university for 10 years; yet, they are not full-time employees. "Administrators understand that people don't like the idea of contracted labor. . . . The truth is that all UCLA cares about is profit and the corporations that contribute a huge amount of its revenue" (*Daily Bruin Online* 1-3). This might be true of UCLA, but that institution is not alone. There are many others which have their own scams going.

GREED IN SPORTS:

The Atlantic Coast Conference (ACC) mentioned in chapter three is all about greed—greed among the chancellors and university presidents. Sports Columnist Bob Smizik stated it well, "The ongoing raid of the Big East Conference by the Atlantic Coast Conference is not just another example of the seamy side of college athletics but ample testimony that the presidents and chancellors are waist-deep in this mire" (Smizik 1-3). In an article by Adam Kilgore appearing in *The Daily Orange – Sports* he, too, saw the greed of college athletics raise its ugly head, regarding the ACC deal . . . "the ACC back-stabbed, drenched itself in questionable politics and cut back-room deals, all the while threatening the legitimacy of higher education in the name of cashing in" (Kilgore 1-3).

I remember a few years ago when the University of Florida had scheduled Central Michigan University's football team to come to Gainesville, Florida for a game with the Gators. Anyone who knows anything about football knew that Florida was going to wipe the field with the players of Central Michigan, and that's exactly what happened—54-6. Why were the Chippewa's of Central Michigan sent to Florida to get embarrassed? Two reasons: one the Gators needed a punching bag, and the greed of Central Michigan University— money.

PATENT GREED:

We don't usually see biotech companies such as Genentech, Biogen and Amgen waging legal battles with a university, but that is what happened with Columbia University. Columbia was accused by the aforementioned biotech companies of trying to prolong three patents that expired in 2000 for another 17 years without having made substantive changes in the products. During the lifetime of those patents, Columbia received nearly $300 million in royalties and licensing fees. "The patent fight demonstrates that a university is as able as any corporation to do anything in its power to continue milking an intellectual-property cash cow" (Stix 1).

After Congress passed legislation which facilitated the rapid transfer of technology in 1980, research universities have become active partners with business. "Critics say that universities' quest for dollars—and their partnerships with the private sector—runs the risk of harming the basic academic mission, which is to teach and conduct research" (Cohen 4-5). Ultimately, it's all about universities' bottom lines. Perhaps this linkage between academia and business could be a contributing factor to the development and growth of the student-customer or customer-student concepts.

Chapter Ten

Freeway Flyin' and Airplane Ridin'—
Strange Destinations Ahead

*T*HIS CHAPTER IS DEVOTED TO SELECTIVE anecdotal accounts of some of my academic sharecropping assignments, because most of us, who do this or have done this, pay or have paid our dues in so many ways that have nothing to do with the delivery of quality education. Sometimes just getting there was quite an accomplishment.

Over my many years of sharecropping, I have encountered some things, in retrospect, about which I truly marvel. Now that I have life firmly ensconced in the rearview mirror of my mind's eye, it's hard to believe that I actually lived through some of the bizarre situations I experienced, because the travel alone was enough to hasten premature death. The stress levels, even before September 11, 2001, made flying undesirable and hard work. Just the fact that when you are in a flight status this alone creates tensions and uncertainty about what will happen next. My experience of traveling the highways and byways by car as a "roads scholar" or flying the sometimes not so friendly skies of North America has not been fun, because I'm sure I clocked more downtime in airports than I did classroom time. There have been countless situations in which I have been *stuck* in an airport somewhere, frustrated, and pressured to find a way either to my teaching assignment or to get back home. I think it's fair to say that when travel time is considered, I doubt I earned the minimum wage for a lot of my sharecropping courses. Though the following accounts might sound fictional, they are not. Except for failures of memory, these are accurate anecdotes presented without embellishment.

CEDAR WHERE?

I answered my office phone one December morning and found a university administrator on the other end with whom I had a good relationship.

After the usual pleasantries, he said, "Wendell, I have a couple of teaching assignment options for you."

"What are they?" I asked. He sort of mumbled the first one, and I didn't really catch it. Then, he said the other one was in Coral Springs, Florida.

"What was the first one again?"

"Cedar Rapids, Iowa," he said, hesitatingly.

"Iowa? Gee, that'll be in the middle of winter. I think you know my choice. Let me have Coral Gables."

"You'd really like the classes in Cedar Rapids, they're very studious people, and I know how you are about that," he said almost in a pleading tone. I could tell he needed me to take the assignment, but I really didn't want to go to cold country during the winter. After all, I had been a north Florida resident all my life and usually avoided extremely cold weather, but I didn't want to tell him no. I didn't want to let him down.

"Tell you what, let think on it overnight, and I'll get back with you in the morning."

By the next morning I had reached my decision to accept the two MBA courses in Cedar Rapids. So, as the middle of

January rolled around, I hopped on a plane at Jacksonville International Airport and headed north. We had an intermediate stop in St. Louis, and from there all I could see as I looked down from the plane was nothing but a blanket of snow the rest of the way to Cedar Rapids.

When we landed, it was 10:30 A.M., Central Time and the ground level temperature was six degrees. Though I had dressed for the ungodly cold, I didn't look forward to the outdoors. After we landed, I went to the Avis counter to get my rental. The woman told me to pick up the car just outside of the terminal at space A19, so I grabbed the keys and contract, bundled up, and went outside. I had a slight problem. The lettering was on the ground under several inches of snow, so I went to about where I thought A19 should be and started comparing the tag number listed on the key ring to the cars available, but I wasn't able to immediately locate the car. There was about a 15 mile per hour wind blowing so the effective temperature was well below zero, and I had to be careful because of treacherous footing as I continued the search. Finally, I found the car, but by then, my gloved hands felt like ice and I was cold to the bone. I tried the key in the door but had trouble opening it. I had mental visions of a newspaper headline that said "Florida Man Found Frozen in Avis Parking lot While Clinging to Rental Car Door."

When I left the airport, I took I-380 to downtown Cedar Rapids which I discovered was about six miles away. As I drove I wondered about my decision to go to Cedar Rapids, because I had four more weekends to go after that weekend for a measly $4,000 for the two courses. I checked in at the Five Seasons Hotel which was the only hotel in town which had covered parking. I had plenty of time to rest before my first class, so after I unpacked, that's just what I did.

I left the hotel at 5:00 to go to the teaching site, located only a few miles outside of town. Since I had never been there before, I really didn't know where I was going, but when I got to the campus where the classes were being held, I treaded through the snow and ice to get to the building. It took me a while to locate the classroom, because there was no representative from the school to provide any assistance. Once I finally found the classroom, I also found the university representative. It would have been a courteous gesture for him to have met me at the entrance, but I suppose that would have been asking too much. Little did I know then how lucky I was, because I only got to see him one other time during the next four weekends, and that was for the purpose of having the students complete my student faculty evaluation forms.

The students were everything and more than my friend the administrator had told me, because for the next ten years I returned to Cedar Rapids, Iowa every winter to teach a class or classes until my friend was moved to a different position. After that, a difficult and petty administrator took over who made sure I didn't get an assignment there or anyplace I preferred, because she knew how much I enjoyed teaching and working with the citizens of Cedar Rapids. Besides, she felt threatened by someone who didn't have to work for the university. Once again, power, politics, and pettiness prevailed over doing what was right, just, or fair. Despite that, there really is something about the work ethic of those who are born and reared in the Midwest. They are wonderful people, great students, and I have missed not teaching at that site.

St. Louis Bound!

It was in the dead of winter when my plane landed at Lambert International Airport in St. Louis. I had left the warm climate of Jacksonville, Florida at 7:00 A.M. on a Friday to return to another series of weekend MBA classes in Cedar Rapids, Iowa. My flight was scheduled to leave at 8:30 A.M. Central Time. The operative word was "scheduled" to leave. Any frequent flyer knows that "scheduled" to leave and actually leaving are two very different things.

I appeared at the TWA counter about 30 minutes before we were supposed to board only to find that the flight had been cancelled. The agent put me on another flight which was scheduled to leave two hours later. I appeared at the next TWA counter to catch my new flight to discover that the plane had a mechanical problem and they were not sure when it would be fixed. After an hour I checked again and was told that that flight, too, had been cancelled. Then, I was booked on the last flight to Cedar Rapids for that day. By now, it was 2:00 P.M. and I had walked the entire terminal two or three times. When I returned to the TWA counter, the flight attendant informed me that the flight would not be leaving because the airport in Cedar Rapids had been closed because of ice and snow. Then, I began scrambling for a flight to the nearest airport to Cedar Rapids. I was ready and willing to go to Moline, Illinois or wherever it made sense, but flight after flight had been cancelled to surrounding cities because of the inclement weather.

I knew by then that there was no way I was going to be able to get to my class by 6:00 P.M. that day, so I attempted to contact someone back on the campus in Florida to get further instructions. After an hour of attempting to get the correct person on the phone, I finally gave up. I was thinking about just catching a flight back to Jacksonville and just forget it when a man walked up to me and asked if I would be willing to rent a car and drive to Cedar Rapids. He introduced himself as the former CEO of the Amana Corporation which is located near Cedar Rapids. He said if I would drive that he would navigate, since he knew an efficient route. I agreed and we headed north. The weather was terrible; nothing but rolling fog, and even some rain accompanied us for the first couple of hours. After a while we began dealing with snow. The roads we took were dark and dangerous, but we forged ahead.

We didn't get to his house in the Amana Colonies until nearly 7:00 P.M., and I still had an hour to drive to get to the hotel in Cedar Rapids. Once I got there, I was unable to contact the university representative, so I had some dinner and went to bed. The next morning I drove out of the hotel garage and gingerly crept up the on ramp of I-380. Though the trucks had come through with salt and sand, there was a lot of black ice and the highway was treacherous. I drove along at about 40 miles per hour as I looked from side to side of the freeway. Over the next five miles I counted more than a dozen cars and trucks in the ditches on either side of the road. I was thankful that I was a southern boy, because I knew that a person couldn't drive as usual under such road conditions, but many of those indigenous to the area tried to be cavalier and drive the way they always did.

When I got to my first class, I explained my absence the night before and they understood. Unlike me, they were used to the foibles of the weather. That was one of the most stressful sharecropping trips I can ever recall.

YOU CAN'T GET THERE FROM HERE

Once again, it was during the winter when a different university asked me to go to a small town in North Carolina to teach a graduate course in administrative business strategy. This was a better deal than the university which had employed me for the Cedar Rapids MBA courses, because I only had to teach on three weekends instead of five, and I was paid $2,500 for the course.

The travel people for the university made me an airline ticket reservation which was to take me to Fayetteville, North Carolina from Jacksonville, Florida. I left Jacksonville International Airport on a December Friday morning for my intermediate stop in Atlanta, Georgia, and anyone who lives in the south knows that it's nearly impossible to go anywhere by plane without going through Atlanta, Georgia. I've had to go through Atlanta so many times that I believe when I die I will be shipped to the airport in Atlanta, and my cold dead body will be rolled into the Delta Crown Room near gate A16—just so someone can tag my toe.

After our arrival in Atlanta, I proceeded to the Fayetteville gate for my next flight, where I was informed by the ticket agent that a heavy snow storm had swept through North Carolina, and the flight could not go into the airport at Fayetteville. I listened intently to my option, "You really can't get there from here, but we can get you to the Raleigh Airport, because it's still open," she said. Of course, what else was I to do? So, I was rebooked to Raleigh, even though I knew it took me out of my way. I finally arrived at the snow-blanketed airport around midday, and headed to Avis to get my rental car. When I got to the counter the fun began, because the university had reserved me a car in Fayetteville, not Raleigh. This became a monumental problem, because I didn't have a car reserved in Raleigh, and the agency had to look hard to find me an available vehicle. After nearly an hour of wrangling, I got a set of keys and a contract and went outside the terminal into an abundance of ice and snow. I actually had to hold on to stationary objects in order to locate the car.

When I finally made my way up on the Interstate that circled the Raleigh Triangle, the snow was so deep I couldn't find road signs and other landmarks of distinction. I drove incessantly, but I couldn't find highway 70 east. After a while, I realized I had circled around Raleigh twice and was on my third round when I decided to do everything the opposite way, then all of a sudden I thought I saw what might be the turnoff, so I made the turn, and soon found out it was the right decision. I traveled for hours over very treacherous terrain before I finally arrived at the hotel where I was to stay. I was late for the class which was supposed to begin at 6:00 P.M., so I contacted the university representative to let her know I had arrived. It was then that she told me she had made the decision to cancel the class for that evening, because she thought the snow storm would preclude me from making it to the class that weekend.

She then had to re-contact the students to let them individually know we would be having class the next morning.

The next morning I drove to the hospital where the classes were being held, and discovered that three of the students did not get the message that we would be having class; however, I pressed on with the duties at hand. By noon the other three finally showed up. Before the weekend was over, I was able to make an observation about the quality of the students which proved to be accurate by the end of the course—they, as a class, were not graduate material. I'm sure that was not a concern of the university, because they were receiving $750.00 for each of the 15 students for a gross amount of $11, 250. After my pitiful pay and expenses they were able to net well over $6,000.

THE ICE AND SNOW LOVED ME

I was hired by this same university for another job in North Carolina where the snow and ice chased me down again, but not until after I got to the city where the course was to be taught. I arrived at my hotel on a Friday afternoon, but I could tell bad weather was on the way. The classes were to be held on a military installation. Sometime during the night a full-fledged ice storm, along with some snow, covered the city and countryside. Saturday morning I tried to leave the hotel to drive to the class, but I couldn't. The ice was so thick and heavy I nearly didn't get to the car in the parking lot. After I did get into the car, I tried to leave the parking lot, but the car just slid along out of control, so I parked it and carefully made my way back into the hotel. I called the university representative and told her about the situation. We mutually agreed to try again on Sunday morning.

Since the lousy hotel that the travel people had booked me in didn't have a restaurant, I couldn't get anything to eat. But, by late afternoon, hunger drove me from the hotel, even though I couldn't drive to a restaurant. I took a chance and left on foot. On my trek a number of times I nearly fell, but I kept going until I found an open restaurant a few blocks away.

The next morning was no better than the first, and we could not convene class. Worse still, I found out that the airport runways were unusable so I couldn't catch my flight back to north Florida. I called the Delta ticket office at the airport and they booked me on a flight out of Florence, South Carolina. By noon I was able to drive the car very slowly, but I must admit with great trepidation. About an hour outside of Fayetteville the ice had disappeared and several hours later I made my connection in Florence.

A troublesome issue that surfaced was the cancelled class had to be rescheduled so that the students would get the benefit of all three weekends. I had no problem with that, but I had wasted an entire weekend and never received a penny for it—once again, so much for fairness.

HELPING OTHERS OUT—NOT ALWAYS A GOOD IDEA

Right after Jeb Bush was first elected as governor of Florida I received a call from an administrator of an institution for which I had taught many courses. She was head and shoulders above most of the administrators with whom I had worked, regardless of the institution. She called me and asked if I could help her out, because she was in a bind. She explained that a full-time faculty member had suddenly quit the university to join Governor Bush's new administration. That faculty member was scheduled to teach two sections of a graduate course in human resource management twice a week on Tuesday and Thursday mornings for 16 weeks.

I explained I was several hundred miles away and didn't know how I could help. She said that the university could fly me to the site in the early morning twice a week and then back in the afternoon. I told her to give me a day or so, and I would get back with her because I had to look at my schedule and see if I could make it work.

The next day I talked with an associate of mine and asked if he could help me out when and where I had previous obligations, and he was able to accommodate me, so I called her back and agreed to give it a shot. The pay for the two courses wasn't much—only $4,000, but I wanted to help if I could.

I caught a Southwest Airline flight at 7:00 A.M. twice a week for 16 weeks and then back again in the early afternoon. By the time I was about halfway through the term, I was physically and mentally exhausted, but I hung in there and got the job done. Between the two classes, I had 51 students, and it amounted to a great deal of work, that is, if you are a dedicated and responsible teacher and believe that the students should be served well. I have always viewed the lecture and instruction part of the course to be the easy part. It's what I call the administrative duties and responsibilities, e.g., the annotating, evaluating, and grading of papers and the writing and grading of exams so that the students will receive feedback about their performance which has tremendous significance. Until that is done, the job is not over.

After the term was over, I examined the financial aspects of the deal. The students, 51 of them, paid $1,500 each for the course which was a gross of $76,500 for the university. I actually ended up receiving an extra $2,000 as a bonus, because the administrator insisted that I be recognized for making the sacrifice that I did. When I got the extra money, the Associate Dean acted as though he was doing *me* a favor. Obviously, I netted less than the $6,000 they paid me, and I found out later that the full-time faculty member which I replaced had an annual salary of $58,000 before she resigned. When my pay and expenses were factored, the university netted approximately $71,000, because I am an academic sharecropper and, in some ways, a fool. Thank God I will never do something like that again.

Sarasota Via Miami

Several years ago I was hired to teach a graduate course in Sarasota, Florida. At the time I was living in Jacksonville, Florida, so it was only a hop, skip, and jump to the teaching site. That was a time when Florida still had some decent intrastate air service—unlike today. Now, the best way to get around the state is by automobile.

I arrived at the Jacksonville International Airport at about 10:00 A.M., so that I would have plenty of time to get to Sarasota, because I was supposed to begin class at 6:00 P.M. Our aircraft was due to depart at eleven o'clock, so as I was sitting in my seat looking out at the wing section, I noticed a pool of oil which had dripped down onto the tarmac. The plane was a turboprop EMB-120 that Delta used a lot during the 1990s. I didn't like the looks of what I saw, so I informed the flight crew that there was a problem that needed to be investigated. The pilot and the copilot took a quick walk around and concurred and the maintenance crew was summoned. We all disembarked and waited inside the terminal for the verdict. After about an hour it was determined that the plane was not fit for flight, and Delta did not have another flight to Sarasota that day, so the scramble began. After hassling with the ticket agents about other carriers and substitute flights, I went to the United Airlines ticket counter to get booked on a flight going south, but not to Sarasota. The only flight United had was to Miami, but it wasn't scheduled to leave until four o'clock, so I had them book me. I knew right then I would never make it to Sarasota in time for my class at six, so I made a call to the university representative on campus and told them the situation. They said they would advise the site administrator in Sarasota that the Friday night class would have to be cancelled and that the Saturday morning class would go on as planned.

After we all had loaded on the United flight which was supposed to leave at four, we were delivered some more bad news. There was a mechanical problem with the plane, and we would have to be rebooked on the last flight to Miami which was scheduled to leave at nine o'clock. By this time I had spent nine hours in the airport and had gone nowhere. I kept thinking I could easily have driven to Sarasota in less than six hours.

The flight did leave on time and we landed around ten-thirty in Miami. By the time I got my rental car it was eleven o'clock. As I exited the airport I looked for signage which told me which way to turn, but I didn't see anything, so I guessed which way to go. As soon as I came to the first toll booth I asked the attendant if I was going in the right direction, and she assured me I was. I traveled for about another 30 minutes and realized I was going in the wrong direction. I was headed south toward the Keys. I got off the turnpike and went back the way I had come. I entered the Alligator Alley part of the turnpike, and for the next hour and a half I only counted six cars heading south.

I finally got to my hotel at two-thirty in the morning, and I immediately fell asleep, but I had to get up at six so that I could get to the class by eight. That was a memorable, long weekend, and I'm sure that when my travel time was factored, I wasn't even earning minimum wage, and I only had four more weekends to go to earn my pitiful $2,000.

The anecdotes related above are only a handful of such experiences. There are many more which stand out in my mind, but I don't want to tire the reader. My hope is to show the sacrifice that men and women like me make or have made as academic sharecroppers.

Epilogue

*I*F THERE IS ANY QUESTION ABOUT WHY I THINK THIS BOOK is important; let me be specific about it. The overriding purpose of this work was to inform and educate people about the lack of conscience, moral compass, and ethical framework upon which to build the higher education industry. Is the industry amoral, i.e., morality neutral? If it is, it should not be. I and We have toiled in these fields of academia as sharecroppers out of love for teaching and the need to earn a living—without being appreciated or rewarded appropriately. The time has long since passed that the exploitation of adjunct faculty stop. Moreover, students, the system, and the general public deserve better.

What I've tried to do is to show that there is an immense problem in higher education, and something needs to be done to rectify the moral and ethical breaches by those who hold positions of power. Leaders and administrators of higher education have an obligation to stop playing the games of power, politics, and pettiness through the exploitation of the system. Professionals' careers and lives are affected in a very negative way. Most of these people are good human beings who make significant contributions to their respective institutions who end up being manipulated and abused by those who hold the power.

My call for needed change will be considered by many to be naïve or Pollyannaish, but I have faith in humanity. I believe that humanity, at the core, is good. Admittedly, though as an academic sharecropper, I really don't have a lot of reason to be optimistic, I am an optimist. I believe that the solutions of today often become the problems of tomorrow, and that's why I still have some faith in the system. Back in the 1970s the introduction of large numbers of adjunct faculty seemed to be the solution for the problem of the time, and today adding abundant adjunct faculty is the modality of choice, but now that solution has become problematic. As this practice has grown to where currently nearly half of all courses taught in the United States are taught by adjunct faculty (academic sharecroppers), something should be done about the issue of exploitation. Whether or not my efforts are meaningful will depend on my ability to convince and communicate that change is needed and that a willing educational leadership is ready and able to respond.

To use an old west metaphor, I think and feel like what a lot of older gunslingers must have thought and felt like during the short 20 years of the "wild west" about which there is so much myth and lore. From what I've read, many of them as they became old men at the age of 45 or so didn't want to do it anymore. It wasn't that they couldn't, they didn't want to face down another man, and when they had to they did. In many ways, that's where I am mentally and emotionally. I don't want to *prove* myself to another administrator or student. I don't want to have to face down anyone, but if I have to I can, and if an epiphany does occur in higher education, which is highly unlikely as mentioned earlier in this book, perhaps I'll dust off my book bag and brief case and give it another try.

Finally, I would be remiss if I did not speak to and thank the thousands of students in hundreds of classes I taught during my tenure as their instructor at a variety of times and in varied places and settings. I have been blessed with meeting these bright and engaging people, many of whom touched my life and I theirs.

Works Cited

About Distance Learning. "Hidden Online Course Costs," <http://distancelearn.about. com/cs/financialaid/a/ aa072803.htm> (October 7, 2004).

Andersen, John O. "Why We Should Question Our Support of the Higher Education Industry," <http://www. spiritone.com (August 31, 2004).

Arnone, Michael. "Students Face Another Year of Big Tuition Increases in Many States," <http://chronicle.com [Section: Government & Politics, Volume 49, Issue 49, Page A24>] (8/31/2004).

Atkinson, Roark. "Adjunct Faculty: A Buyer's Market," *Organization of American Historians*,http://www.oah. org/pubs/n1/96nov/adjunct1196.htm (September 24, 2004).

Avakian, Nancy A. "Increasing Reliance on Adjunct Faculty Members," <http:// Leahi.kcc.hawaii.edu/org/tcc_ conf96/avajuab.html> (August 18, 2004).

Berry, David A. "Community Colleges and Part-Time and Adjunct Faculty," <http:// www.oah.org/pubs/commcoll/berry.html >. Copyright © 1999 The Organization of American Historians ISBN 1-884141-03-X (August 18, 2004).

Boettcher, Judith. "Online Course Development: What Does It Cost," (from Campus Technology – 7/1/2004)

<http://www.campus-technology.com/print. asp?ID=9676> (October 7, 2004).

Botch, Carol Sears & Botch, Robert E. "Gaining Faculty Acceptance for Online Courses at a Traditional College," (from CASE STUDIES) July/August 2000 <http:// ts.mivu.org.default.asp?show=article&id=788> (October 24, 2004).

Bricault, Dennis. "Penny Wise and Pound Foolish? The Financial Implications of Adjunct Faculty," North Park University, November, 1998. <http://campus. northpark.edu/esl/adjunct.html#hist> (August 18, 2004).

Budd, Mike. *"Degrees of Shame:* Adjuncts and GAs Organize," copyright 2001, *Jump Cut: A review of Contemporary Media,* No. 44, Fall 2001. <http:// www.ejumpcut.org/archive/jc44.2001/Budd/ templabortext.html> (September 3, 2004).

Carnevale, Dan. "Professors Seek Compensation for Online Courses," (from *The Chronicle of Higher Education* – Information Technology August 13, 2004) http://chronicle.com.free.v50/i49/49a02701.htm (October 7, 2004).

Chaney, Michael Alexander. "An Academic Exorcism" (A review in *Post modern Culture, PMC* 10.1, copyright 1999). http://nersp.nerdc.ufl.edu/lombardi (September 3, 2004).

Chernow, Elizabeth. "Adjunct Faculty Look to Unionize," *GW Hatchet – Campus News,* Issue: 3/11/04, http://www.gwhatchet.com/global_user_elements/ (August 18, 2004).

CNN – "ValuJet Crash Case in Hands of Jury," <http://www. cnn.com/1999/US/12/02/ Valujet.crash.02/.

Cohen, Warren. "Taking Care of Business," (from *Prism Online* – January 2000) <http:// www.prism-magazine.org/jan00/html/coverstory.cfm> (October 29, 2004).

Cornell University. "Cornell study finds student ratings
soar on all measures when professor uses more
enthusiasm: study raises concerns about the validity
of student evaluations," (from *Science News* –
September 19, 1997 – contact: Susan Lang at e-mail:
SSL4@cornell.edu)
http://www.news.cornell.edu/releases/ Sept 97/
student.eval.ssl.html> (October 17, 2004).

Crumbley, D. Larry. "The Dysfunctional Atmosphere
of Higher Education: Games Professors Play,"
[*Accounting Perspectives* – spring 1995, Vol. 1, No. 1]
http://www.bus.lsu.edu/accounting/faculty/lcrumbley/
behavior.html (October 31, 2004).

Daily Bruin Online. "Casual workers pay price for university's
greed," (from *Daily Bruin Archives* – May 17, 2000)
http://www.dailybruin.ucla.edu/db/archivesdarticles.
Asp?ID=433&date=...> (October 29, 2004)

Daughenbaugh, Richard; Ensminger, David; Frederick,
Lynda; & Surry, Daniel. "Does Personality Type
Effect Online Versus In-Class Course Satisfaction?"
Seventh Annual Mid-South instructional Technology
Conference, April 7-9, 2002.<http://www.mtsu.edu/
itconf/proceed02/3.html> (October 4, 2004).

Delaney, Bill. "Second-class careerists? The Long Halls of
Ivy: Adjunct Professors.
http://www.cnn.com/2001/CAREER/trends/01/02/
adjunct. January 1, 2001.

Dick, Anthony. "A 'Star Chamber' on Grounds,"
<http://www.cavalierdaily.com/CV Article_print.
asp?ID=19567&pid1144> (October 22, 2004).

Distance-Educator.com. "New Poll Shows Faculty Prefer
Web-Enhanced Courses to Either Classroom-Only
or Distance-Only Courses," (from *Higher Education
/ Daily News*) April 17, 2001, <http:www.distance-
educator.com/dnews> (October 4, 2004).

Distance Learning. "The New Education Wave of the

Future," <http://www. thelearningweb.net/distance-learning.html (October 5, 2004).

Downes, Stephen, "Future of OnlineLearning,"<http://www. downes.ca/future/economics. htm> (October 7, 2004).

Draper, Joe. "Coaches Receive Both Big Salaries and Big Questions," (January 1, 2004) http://www.nytimes.com2004/01/01sports/ ncaafootball/01SALA.html... (November 11, 2004).

Dresner, Jonathan. "Grade Inflation . . . Why it's a Nightmare," (from *Historians/History* 8-02-04) <http://hnn.is/articles/6591.html> (October 16, 2004).

Dubson, Michael (Editor) *Ghosts in the Classroom: Stories of College Adjunct Faculty—and the Price We All Pay* (from *the Montana professor* 14.1 Fall 2003) <http:// mtprof.msun.edu/Fall2003/charrev.html> (September 24, 2004).

Earl, James. "Faculty Voice—Profit Quest Not Worth Sacrifice of Education," Dated June 18, 2001, http://www.ncaa.org/news/2001/20010702/comment. html> (September 20, 2004).

Economicprincipals.com. "Going to Trial?" David Walsh Editor, October 27, 2002 http://www.economicprincipals.com/issues/02.10.27. html (October 22, 2004).

Eisenstadt, Marnie & Weaver, Teri. "College Has Become a Big Business," *The Post- Standard,* September 1, 2004 <http://www.syracuse.com/news/poststandard/ Index.ssf?base/news-0/1> (September 10, 2004).

Elearnspace.org. "Elearning vs. Classrooms," (from elearnspace everything elearning) September 24, 2002 <http://www.elearnspace.org/Articles/Week1_ Elearningvs. Classrooms.htm> (October 4, 2004).

Elliott, Jim. "Guest Opinion: Cheapest Way Isn't Best Way for Montana," <http://www.matr.net/print-6214.html> (August 31, 2004).

Emery, Charles; Kramer, Tracy; & Tian, Robert. "Return

to Academic Standards: Challenge the Student Evaluation of Teaching Effectiveness," (October 16, 2004).

Falkenberg, Steve. "Grade Inflation," copyright 1996 <http:// www/sbs.eku.edu/PSY/ FALKENBE/grdinfla.htm> (October 16, 2004). *Fox News.* Broadcast aired 12:30 P.M., Saturday September 25, 2004. *Fox News.* Broadcast aired 6:30 P.M., Friday November 12, 2004.

Frey, Alan. "Busting the Myths About Plight of Part-time Faculty," *CCA Advocate*, Vol. 37, No. 2, Mar/Apr 2002, <http://www.cta.org/Higher Education/v37n2/ article_ 7.htm> (September 24, 2004).

Fulton, Richard D. "The Plight of Part-timers in Higher Education," Looksmart, <http:// www.findarticles.com/p/articles/mi_m1254/ is_3_32/ai_62828426/... (September 24, 2004).

George Mason. "Quality of Work Life," http://www.gmu.edu/ qwl/comm (September 3, 2004).

Goode, Erica. "Incompetence is bliss, say researchers," (from the *New York Times* – 01/26/2000) <http://www. lingsoft.fi/ reriksso/competence.html> (October 23, 2004).

Goral, Tim. "At All Costs," *University Business* <http://www. universitybusiness.com/ pageprint.dfm?p=526> (September 20, 2004).

Halfond, Jay A. "Grade Inflation is not a victimless crime," (from *The Christian Science Monitor-* May 3, 2004) <http://www/csmonitor.com/2004/0503/p09s01-coop. htm> (October 16, 2004).

Haynes, Scott. "The ACC – A Super Conference?"<http:// www.sportsnetwork.com/ default.asp?c=sportsnewwo rk&page=cf...> (September 20, 2004).

Hodes, Greg P. "Letter to Kansas City Star," dated 6/20/00 (September 3, 2004).

Hosmer, LaRue Tone. *The Ethics of Management.* 4th

Edition, McGraw-Hill Irwin, 2003.

Huemer, Michael. "Are student evaluations a good idea?" (from *Marginal Revolution* – October 2003) <http://www.marginalrevolution.com/marginalrevolution/2003/09/ are_st...> (October 17, 2004).

Iowa State University. "ISU Economics Researcher Shows University's Research Park Provides Economic Boon to Iowa," <http://www.Iastate.edu/nscentral/releases//2003/mar/researchparl.shtml> (September 11, 2004).

Issues & Views. "Complaints, suspensions and condemnation," [*Reprinted from issues & views November 5, 2001*] <http://www.issues-views.com/index.php/sect/21000/ article/21017> (October 29, 2004).

Issues & Views, "Fraud and incompetence: This wasn't supposed to happen here," http://www.issues-views.com/index.php/sect/21000/article/21032 (October 23, 2004).

Johnson, Debbie, Burnett, Michael, & Rolling, Peggy. "Comparison of Internet and Traditional Classroom Instruction in a Consumer Economics Course," *Journal of Family and Consumer Sciences Education,* Vol. 20, no. 2, Fall/Winter 2002.

JUMP CUT: A Review of Contemporary media. "Structural Causes," <http://www.ejumpcut.org/archive.jc44.2001/Budd/templabor2.html> (September 3, 2004).

Kaye, Larry. "Should Full-time Faculty Support the Unionization efforts of Adjunct Faculty?" NEA Higher Education – *Advocate Online,* October 2003 <http://www.nea.org/he/advo03/advo1003/dialog.html> (September 24, 2004).

Kilgore, Adam. "ACC expansion exposes greed of college athletics," *The Daily Orange – Sports,* Issue: 8/25/03 <http://www.dailyorange.com/global_user_elements/print page.cfm?story...> (October 29, 2004).

Kindred, Jeanette. "Thinking About the Online Classroom:

Evaluating the 'Ideal' Versus the 'Real'" <http://www. acjournal.org/holdings/vol3/Iss3/rogue4/ Kindred. html> (October 4, 2004).

Laskey, Kathryn Blackmond. "Are Students Our Customers in the Education Marketplace?" (from the *Mason Gazette* of George Mason University) <http:// www.gmu.edu/news/gazette/9811/studcus.html> (October 28, 2004).

Leiter, Brian. "The Leiter Reports: Editorials, News, Updates," of March 3, 2004 <http:// webapp.utexas. edu/blogs/bleiter.archieves/000890.html> (October 23, 2004).

Leland, Ted. "Vantage Point: Division I College Athletics: A crisis of Core Values," <http://news-service.stanford.edu/news/2003/ november5/vantage-115.html> (September 20, 2004).

Lorenzen, Michael. "Organizational Culture and Institutional Transformation," (from ERIC Digest – August 6, 2004) http://eric-digest.blogspot.com/2004/08/ Organizational-culture-and.html> (October 31, 2004).

Mansfield, Harvey C. "Grade Inflation: It's Time to Face the Facts," (from *The Chronicle of Higher Education* – April 6, 2001) <http://chronicle.com/free/ V47/i30/ 30b02401.htm> (October 16, 2004).

Markatos, Dennis. "Democracy and Tuition Imperiled by Big Business," <http://www. Dailytarheel.com> (August 31, 2004).

Marklein, Mary Beth. "A call for an end to grade inflation," *USA TODAY* - 02/05/2002 http://www.usatoday.com/news/health/2002-02-05-grade-inflation.htm (October 16, 2004).

McArdle, Elaine. "The Adjunct Explosion," <http://www. universitybusiness.com/page. Cfm?p=159> (September 3, 2004).

McGuff, Joe. "Are Big-Time College Athletics Damaging the Integrity of Our Educational System?"

MIDSCONTINENT PERSPECTIVES, <u>Midwest research Institute</u>, March 21, 1989, (retrieved September 20, 2004).

Merrow, John. "Grade Inflation: It's Not Just an Issue for the Ivy League," (from *Carnegie Perspectives*—A different way to think about teaching and learning – June 2004) <http://www.carnegiefoundation.org/perspectives/ perspectives2004. June...> (October 16, 2004).

Millman, M. "Mass Invasion of Privacy" & "Academia at its Worst – LaGuardia Community College Math Department," (11/14/00 & 5/17/00, respectively. <u>http://maxpages.com/lagcorruption/Nov_14_2000</u> and <u>http://maxpages.com/lag</u> corruption/may_17-2000>.

Montell, Gabriela. "Do Good Looks Equal Good Evaluations?" (from *The Chronicle of Higher Education* – October 15, 2003) <http://chronicle.com/ cgi2-bin/printable. cgi?article=http://chronicle.com/...> (October 17, 2004).

Morrison, James L. "Transforming Educational Organizations," <http://horizon.unc.edu/ Projects/ OTH/5-1.asp> (October 31, 2004).

Moser, Richard. The New Academic Labor System, Corporatization and the Renewal of Academic Citizenship. (American Association of University Professors) <http://www.aaup.org/Issues/part-time/ cewmose.htm (September 3, 2004).

Moy, Geri. "The Effectiveness of the Virtual Classroom in Higher Education,"
<http:// <u>www.towson.edu/users/gmoy/virtual classroom.html</u>> October 4, 2004).

Myers Online. "Is Taking an Online Course at Myers Less Demanding Than the Classroom?" <u>http://www.dnmyers.edu/online/demand_on_the_ student.html</u> (October 4, 2004).

Pelletier, Jen. "Students see grade problems at BU," (from *The Daily Free Press* – January 14, 2004) <http://

www.dailyfreepress.com/news/2004/01/14/News/
Students.See.G...> (October 16, 2004).

Penner, Jonathan. "Grade Inflation: Causes, Consequences,
Cures," <http://www. u.arizona.edu/ ctb/cogdoc01.
html> (October 16, 2004).

Phillips, Vicky. "Internet Changing Economics of Higher
Education," (from CNN.com) May 5, 1999 http://
www.cnn.com/TECH/computing/9905/05/neted.itg
(September 11, 2004).

Rau, A. Ravi P. & Bell, Paul. "Infectious Greed," <http://
www.bus.lsu.edu/accounting/ Faculty/lcrumbley/
InfectGreed.htm> (October 29, 2004).

Redovich, Dennis W. "180 The Greed and Self Interests of
American Universities," Center for the Study of Jobs
& Education in Wisconsin and the United States -
November 2003.

RightNow Technologies. "University of Memphis: University
of Memphis eliminates inefficiencies and enters the
digital future with RightNow," <http://www.right now.
com/resource/casestudy.php?id=1030> (October 30,
2004).

Rombeck, Terry. "Athletics Arms Race: Programs'
Successes Tied to Money," *KU News*, December 7,
2003. <http://www.kusports.com/news/kunews/story/
108749> (September 20, 2004.

Ross, Philip. "Stifling of Debate Is Detrimental to University,"
(from *The Tower Online* – Catholic University of
America, 9/24/2004)
http://cuatower.com/news/2003/02/07 /Forum.Stifling.
Of.Debate....> (October 22, 2004).

Safetylogic.com. "Safetylogic Online Employee Training,"
<http://www.saftetylogic. Com/tour/OET_tour12.asp>
(October 4, 2004).

Sandals, Inger. "Part-time Faculty Gaining Strength
as Numbers Rise," (from *Arizona Star,* Tucson,
Arizona; Aug 8, 2001) <http://iwhome.com/aaup/

advocate102001/ Part-time.htm> (August 18, 2004).

Shapiro, Mark H. (The Irascible Professor™) "Irreverent Commentary on the State of Education in American Today," copyright 1999<http://irascibleprofessor.com/com/comments-12-26-99.htm> (October 17, 2004).

"Sharecropper," <http://www.ddc2000.com/products/samples/ss2kwebdemo/grade5/ Supp...> (July 28, 2004).

Simmons, T. L. "Student Evaluation of Teachers: Professional Practice or Punitive Policy?" (from *Shiken: JALT Testing & Evaluation SIG Newsletter*, Vol. 1, No. 1, October 1996 – p. 12-16.

Slavin, David H. "Part-Time Labor and a Profession in Crisis," (from *Radical Historians Newsletter* No. 83, December 2000) <http://chnm.gmu.edu/rhr.rhn/no83/slavin. Htm (September 24, 2004).

Smith, Lawrence N., [Executive Editor] "Quality Customer Service-Student Retention and Institutional Viability," Valdosta State University <http://services.valdosta.edu/excellence/quality.htm (October 28, 2004).

Smizik, Bob. "Smizik: College Athletics Get Poor Grades on Standards," *Post-gazette.com* Sports. <http://www.post-gazette.com/sports/columnists/20010702 smizik0702p...> (September 20, 2004).

Smizik, Bob. Smizik: Presidents' greed fuels ACC's Raid," *Post-Gazette.com Sports* –May 19, 2003 <http://www.post-gazette.com/sports/columnists/2003051 smizik 0519p...> (October 29, 2004).

Solidarity Forever, "Cogs in the Classroom Factory: The Changing Identity of Academic Labor," Reviewed by Alan G. Heffner and edited by Deborah Herman and Julie Schmid. *The NEA Higher Education Journal,* Thoughts and Action, Winter 2004.

Steiner, George & Steiner, John. *Business, Government, and Society: A Managerial Perspective Text and Cases*, Tenth Edition, McGraw-Hill Irwin, 2003.

Stix, Gary. "Working the System II: Corporate greed

no longer remains the sole domain of the Corporation," *Scientific American.com* – February 9, 2004<http://www.sciam.com/print_version. cfm?articleID=000790A0-C61F> (October 29, 2004).

Student As Customers. (from OCAIR Group discussion) <http://www.ocair.org/files/ Knowledgebase/ PolicyIssue/StAsCustomer.htm> (October 28, 2004).

Student Evaluations: A Critical Review. <http://home.sprynet. com/ Dowl1/sef.htm> (October 21, 2004).

Suhrbur, Tom. "Adjunct Faculty Association of Chicago, IEA-NEA," <http://www. Chicagococoal.org/AFACstrategy. htm > (August 18, 2004).

Tallahassee Democrat. "Research Facility Boon for the State," <http://www.tallahassee. Com/mld/democrat/ news/local/6977487.htm> (September 11, 2004).

Tenser, James. "UA Sports Generate Tens of Millions for Tucson. How Big Is the Game?" *Inside Tucson Business,*<http://www.azbiz.com/AXBIZ/0905edition/ myarticles997...(September 20, 2004).

The Committee on Energy and Commerce, Joe Barton, Chairman U.S. House of Representatives (Prepared Statement of the Honorable Cliff Stearns) <http:// energycommerce.house.gov/108/Hearings/ 03112004hearing 1226 . . . (September 20, 2004).

The Pace Press. "Students are victims of the University's financial incompetence," March 24, 2004 <http://www. pacepress.org/news/2004/03/24/Editorial/Students. Are.Vic...> (October 23, 2004).

Tortorano, David. "Higher Education is Big Business," *The Sun Herald* Gulfport, Mississippi, November 6, 2002 (August 31, 2004).

Trout, Paul A. "Flunking the Test: The Dismal Record of Student Evaluations," [His e-mail address is trout@english.montana.edu.] (October 17, 2004).

Trout, Paul A. "Low Marks for Top Teachers," *Washington Post, March 13, 2000 pg. A17*

http://econc10.bu.edu/Decline/stud_eval_b.htm
(October 31, 2004).

Trummel, Paul. "Whores of Academe – Introduction,"
copyright 1997, All rights Reserved: 11 Feb
97/14:48 PST, Edition: #603-00-00/03-0928-1104
<Webspinner@ContraCabal.org> (October 22, 2004).

University Times. "Turning the Tables: The importance of
student evaluations of faculty varies," (The faculty and
staff newspaper of the University of Pittsburgh) Vol.
34, No. 18, May 16, 2002
http://www.pitt.edu/utimes/issues/34/020516/10.html
(October 21, 2004).

Vilic, Boris. "Online Course Caps: A Survey," (from *Campus
Technology*, 7/1/2004)
http://www.campus-technology.com/article.
asp?id=9679 (October 7, 2004).

Wallace, Jim B. "The Case for Student as Customer,"
(QICID: 13377) (from American Society for Quality)
Series: Quality Progress, Vol. 32, No. 2, February
1999, pp. 47-51,
http://qic.asq.org/perl/search.pl?item=13377 (October
28, 2004).

Wiesberg, Steve. "Top college coaches getting top dollar,"
(*USA TODAY* – 8/3/2001) (November 11, 2004).

Wilson, Carol. "A Tale of Two Classes: Face-to-Face Versus
Online," (from Seventh Annual Mid-South Instructional
Technology Conference – The Connected Classroom,
April 7-9, 2002 <http://www.mtsu.edu/ itconf/
proceed02/70.html> (October 4, 2004).

Wilson, Robin. "New Research Casts Doubt on Value of
Student Evaluations of Professors: Studies find that
faculty members dumb down material and inflate
grades to get good reviews," (from *The Chronicle of
Higher Education* – 1998)
http://chronicle.com/colloquy/98/evaluation/
background.htm (October 21, 2004).

Werry, Chris. "The work of Education in the Age of E-College," (*Firstmonday* a peer- reviewed journal on the Internet) <http:www.firstmonday.dk/issues6_5/ werry/> Vol., 6, number 5, May 2001, (August 31, 2004).

Women in Cell Biology. "Is There Gender Bias in Student Evaluation of Teaching?" [WICB Section Editor: Laura Williams, <law@mendel.berkeley.edu>] (October 17, 2004).

Young, Jeffrey. "Duke Professor Releases Data on Grade Inflation at 34 Colleges," (from *The Chronicle of Higher Education: Daily News* 01/30/2003) <http:// Chronicle.com/cgi1-bin/printable.cgi?article=http:// chronicle.com> (October 16, 2004).

Yudof, Mark G. "Total Quality: myth or management in universities?" <http://www.Findarticles.com/p/articles/ mi_m1254.is_n6_v28/ai_190876> (October 31, 2004).

Zlatos, Bill. "Universities, Foundations Become City's Big Business,"<http://www. pittsburghlive.com/x/search/ print_151661.html> (September 13, 2004).

Index

Suhrbur, Tom 147
Supreme Court appointment 9
symbolic action 38

T

Tallahassee Democrat 33, 147
tax 3
teacher xiv, 12, 15, 53, 54, 60, 89,
    132
teaching vii, viii, xiii, xiv, 2, 7, 10,
    11, 12, 14, 15, 20, 24, 25,
    29, 43, 45, 46, 50, 59, 67,
    69, 70, 71, 72, 73, 74, 81,
    83, 84, 85, 86, 87, 88, 90,
    94, 95, 98, 105, 117, 124,
    125, 126, 133, 135, 144
Tennessee 19, 39
Tenser, James 147
tenure system, tenure track 9, 24,
    52, 58
Tortorano, David 147
Total Quality Management (TQM)
    112
traditional 2, 8, 11, 20, 45, 47, 59,
    60, 61, 64, 65, 67, 78, 114
training 3, 7, 8, 34, 59, 64, 116
Trout, Paul A. 147
Truman, Harry, President 4
Trummel, Paul 148
Tuberville, Tommy 39
tuition, student 3, 5, 21, 30, 41,
    117
TWA Airlines 127

U

U.S. Navy 96, 113
Unethical 1, 27, 44, 54, 97, 107
union 46, 47, 48, 49, 50, 51, 67,
    82
United Airlines 133
University 7, 22, 24, 25, 26, 31,
    32, 33, 35, 36, 37, 38, 39,
    51, 68, 75, 76, 77, 78, 84,
    85, 86, 87, 90, 98, 102, 103,

104, 105, 106, 107, 110,
112, 115, 120, 138, 139,
141, 142, 143, 144, 145,
146, 147, 148
University of Alabama 38
University of Minnesota 39
University of North Florida 7
University of Oklahoma 39
University of Phoenix 22, 68
University of Southern Mississippi
    31
University of Tennessee 39
University of Texas 39, 104
University of Washington 39
University of Wisconsin 39
University Partnership Center 98

V

victimization 54
viewership 37
visiting professor 53, 54

W

Wallace, Jim B. 148
Werry, Chris 149
Wiesberg, Steve 148
Wilson, Carol 148
Wilson, Robin 148
Wolf, Barbara 21
wonks, policy 14, 46
workload 84

Y

Young, Jeffrey 149
Yudof, Mark G 149

Z

Zlatos, Bill 149

www.ingramcontent.com/pod-product-compliance
Lightning Source LLC
Chambersburg PA
CBHW020422290526
45785CB00002B/687